The Great Illusionists

The Great Illusionists

Derek Tait

PEN & SWORD
HISTORY

First published in Great Britain in 2018 by
Pen & Sword History
an imprint of
Pen & Sword Books Ltd
47 Church Street
Barnsley
South Yorkshire
S70 2AS

ISBN 978 1 47389 076 3

Typeset in Minion by
Mac Style Ltd, Bridlington, East Yorkshire
Printed and bound in the UK by CPI Group (UK) Ltd,
Croydon, CR0 4YY

Pen & Sword Books Limited incorporates the imprints of Atlas,
Archaeology, Aviation, Discovery, Family History, Fiction, History,
Maritime, Military, Military Classics, Politics, Select, Transport,
True Crime, Air World, Frontline Publishing, Leo Cooper,
Remember When, Seaforth Publishing, The Praetorian Press,
Wharncliffe Local History, Wharncliffe Transport,
Wharncliffe True Crime and White Owl.

For a complete list of Pen & Sword titles please contact
PEN & SWORD BOOKS LIMITED
47 Church Street, Barnsley, South Yorkshire, S70 2AS, England
E-mail: enquiries@pen-and-sword.co.uk
Website: www.pen-and-sword.co.uk

Contents

Acknowledgements

Thanks to John Cox whose wonderful blog 'Wild About Harry' is a great inspiration. John has always been very helpful, friendly and supportive while I've been putting the book together and it's much appreciated. Many thanks also to Kevin Connolly and Marco Pusterla who were both very helpful and lent me some excellent photos and memorabilia from their collections. Thanks also to Mick Hanzlik, Dan Robinson (Weazle Dandaw), Paul Zenon, Paul Kieve, Allan Taylor, Tina Cole and Tilly Barker. Thanks to the many people who have kindly sent me stories, cuttings and photos. I apologise to anyone not mentioned.

Introduction

Long before television, radio and cinema, entertainment could be found at the many music halls and theatres up and down Great Britain. Acts were varied and included singers, comedians, acrobats, dance acts, animal acts, magicians and escapologists as well as male and female impersonators. Shows played to packed audiences. Many people escaped their hum-drum lives, working in cotton mills, coal mines or factories up and down the country, by visiting the local theatre or music hall.

Lions Comiques were as popular in Victorian times as boy bands are today. Smartly dressed young men, known as 'swells' sang songs about the good life and sipping champagne. The most famous of these was George Leybourne whose song 'Champagne Charlie' was as popular as any chart hit today. Other swells included Arthur Lloyd and The Great Vance who sang about fashionable places to be seen. His song 'Walking in the Zoo' popularised the word 'zoo'.

Male and female impersonators drew huge crowds. Vesta Tilley was so convincing with her impersonations that a rumour spread across London that she was actually a man. She became a trendsetter appearing on stage dressed in immaculate Savile Row outfits dressed as sailors, soldiers and policemen.

Speciality acts were many and included one-legged dancers, ventriloquists, trick cyclists, jugglers, fire and sword swallowers as well as slapstick sketches. Magicians and illusionists attracted huge crowds all over the country. Harry Houdini proved a great draw and became the highest earner at the time. He toured Great Britain many times and each time pulled in more and more people to his shows. His act included escapology, illusion and fantasy. His free outdoor stunts would often involve jumping into a local river while bound in chains. Houdini had many imitators and there was a great rivalry between the acts which led to disruption of shows, fist fights and endless challenges.

Illusionists were popular long before Houdini, with Houdini basing himself on a previous illusionist, Robert-Houdin. Illusions could be very elaborate and audiences were more susceptible, believing what they saw, without question, and leaving the theatre overawed by the performance. Many acts were talked about for weeks or months after the artists had left. The thrill of a visit to a music hall or theatre continued until the introduction of the cinema and in particular, the talkies. Houdini continued his act on film, while still touring, while other acts were largely forgotten.

This book includes the stories of the best of the illusionists as well as speciality acts such as Datas and The Human Fly. Some are still well-known names today, while others will be unheard of by many. Marvel at the feats and lives of the Davenport Brothers, The Great Raymond, David Devant, Carl Hertz and Harry Kellar. Relive the tragedies such as the deaths on stage of Chung Ling Soo and the Great Lafayette.

The performers of the late 1800s and early 1900s made way for the many great illusionists and stage artists that we have today. Acts such as David Copperfield, Siegfried and Roy and David Blaine are all influenced by the likes of Houdini, The Great Lafayette and Robert-Houdin and without the innovations of the early artists, the modern performers might not exist. Many of the illusions performed on stage 100 years ago can still be seen in illusionist's acts today.

Including newspaper articles of the day, this book takes you back to an exhilarating time where all entertainment was live and varied and no-one came away disappointed.

Chapter One

The Great Lafayette

The Great Lafayette dressed for his stage performance.

The Great Lafayette was born Sigmund Neuberger in Munich, Germany on 25 February 1871. In 1890, when he was 19 years old, his family emigrated to America. He began his career imitating the act of the Chinese magician, Ching Ling Foo.

He had previously worked in a bank barely making a living wage. He began his stage career as an amateur and left home with just £80 in savings, determined to make a music hall career for himself. His parents had predicted that he would be home within the month without a penny in his pocket. He secured his first engagement at Spokane Falls at a fee of $2 a week. When he asked for this to be increased to $10, he was promptly refused. He told his manager that one day he would make him pay the biggest fee in his record. A few years later, he refused a fee of $250 in the same house. In New Orleans, he managed to save $1,000 and this proved to be the great starting point of his brilliant career. Chicago was the first big city he took by storm followed by New York where, in 1905, he received $5,000 for a twenty three weeks' engagement.

By 1909, Lafayette was touring Great Britain and proved immensely popular. The *Burnley Gazette* of Saturday, 22 May 1909 noted:

> The Great Lafayette has been engaged at an enormous expense to appear at the Burnley Palace Theatre and Hippodrome next week and the management are assured of a crowded house each night. The first series of feats is

An advert for the Great Lafayette's appearance at
the Palace and Hippodrome at Burnley during
May 1909. The show was so popular that he was
engaged to appear for a further six nights. The
performance featured 'The Lion's Den', an act he
was performing when he was tragically killed on
stage.

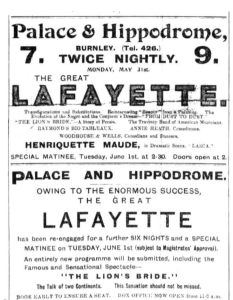

christened a carnival of conjuring and
contains beautiful transformations and
substitutions, reincarnating 'Beauty' from
a painting. The plot, actually performed,
revolves around a sleepy sculptor working
at a model of 'Leda and the Swan.' The
spirit of evil descends and the sculptor
imagines a lump of clay is playing a
lute and finally arouses and finishes his
work. He sees the statue surrounded with cascades of falling waters of the
Fountain of the Isis, sparkling with kaleidoscopic radiance, and then the
statue actually comes to life.

Burnley people are in for a great treat and will pack the house every
evening and at the matinee on Tuesday.

In May 1910, the Great Lafayette was engaged at the Hackney Empire for the holiday
season. He was said to have been their most important music hall engagement
for 'some time past'. It was said that he could catch pigeons in mid-air as if they
had apparently materialised from nowhere, could reincarnate his pet-dog,
Beauty, and evolved human beings
from space, while proclaiming to be
one of the greatest mystery makers
ever known. His programme of
clever illusions was apparently
unlimited with the most effective
item being 'The Sculptor's Dream'.
The versatility of Lafayette was as
remarkable as his performances
were clever and, at the conclusion
of the turn, several excruciatingly
funny travesties on modern musical
conductors were given. At the

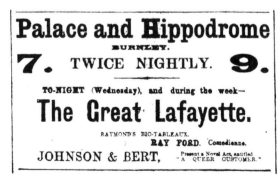

An advert announcing the arrival of the Great
Lafayette at the Palace and Hippodrome in
Burnley in May 1909.

conclusion of the show, the '1912 Overture' was played by the band, and was presented with all the realism and unexpected effects that had made the name of Lafayette pre-eminent amongst the entertainers of the day.

To support Lafayette, there was a strong company of star artistes, including some of the most popular turns on the variety stage at the time. These included the Andos Japs, wonderful acrobats, jugglers, and equilibrists; Ed E Ford, the Australian Sundowner; New Macs, comedians and patterers; The Dandies and the Miles-Stavordale Quintette, who were described as 'expert banjoists'.

Lafayette's shows, including elaborate illusions, were incredibly popular earning him approximately £44,000 a year, the equivalent to about £3.6 million today, making him the most highly paid entertainer of his time.

The Great Lafayette pictured with his dogs.

Lafayette's act included his beloved dog, Beauty, which had been given to him by his friend, Harry Houdini, and travelled with him everywhere. A sign on Lafayette's London home read, 'You may drink my wine; you may eat my food; you may command my servants; but you must respect my dog.'

In the *Portsmouth Evening News* of Monday, 27 March 1911, the Great Lafayette was billed as ' The Man of Mystery'. Acts in his show included the reincarnation

The Great Lafayette with his beloved dog, Beauty. The dog was given to him by his friend, Harry Houdini.

of his dog, Beauty, 'The Mysterious Bathroom', 'Production of Human Beings from Nowhere', 'The Sculptor's Dream', 'From Dust to Dust', 'Travesty Band' and the 'Great Music War Drama 1912'.

A picture of the Great Lafayette which appeared in the *London Daily News* of Thursday, 11 May 1911.

Tragedy struck while Lafayette was playing at the Empire Music Hall in Edinburgh.

He arrived in the city on 30 April 1911 with his dog, Beauty. A day after arriving at the Caledonian Hotel, Beauty died of a stroke. Lafayette was inconsolable. Lafayette announced that his own death wouldn't be far off. He insisted that the dog would have a human burial but was told that the only way that that would happen was if it was buried in the grave of its owner. He bought a plot for himself at Piersfield Cemetery and arranged for Beauty to be buried there on 10 May.

On the evening of 9 May, at 11pm, the Great Lafayette was on stage, performing before an audience of 3,000. He was performing an illusion called 'The Lion's

The stage at the Empire Palace Music Hall where the disastrous fire took place.

A portrait shot of the Great Lafayette.

The Great Lafayette on stage with his dog, Beauty.

The Great Lafayette's troupe performing the illusion 'The Lion's Den' on stage during 1911.

The remains of the Empire Music Hall in Edinburgh after the tragic fire that killed the Great Lafayette in May 1911.

An advert from the *Portsmouth Evening News* of Monday, 27 March 1911 announcing the appearance of the Great Lafayette at the King's Theatre.

Thousands of spectators watched the procession as the Great Lafayette's remains were taken to Piershill Cemetery.

The members of the Great Lafayette's company entering the cemetery.

Bride' which involved a real lion on stage. As the lion roared, a lantern caught fire on the elaborate set. An asbestos fire blanket was brought down. Panic was averted by the conductor who instructed his orchestra to play the National Anthem. This meant that everyone stood up and were quickly ushered to safety.

Behind the curtain, there was panic as the policy of the theatre was that all exits should be locked. There was nowhere to go and several artistes on stage lost their lives. It was reported, at the time, that Lafayette had made it out onto the street but had gone back in to save the lives of both the lion and a black stallion still on stage. This story was later disputed and it was thought that he'd never left the theatre. However, he wasn't seen alive again.

At 5am the next morning, a charred body wearing Lafayette's pasha costume was found beside the dead lion and horse. Two other bodies were recovered which, at the time, were believed to be children but were actually those of two midgets taking part in the show.

The following day, Lafayette's solicitor arrived in Edinburgh and voiced concern that the body found wasn't wearing Lafayette's ostentatious rings. However,

Lafayette's car with two members of his troupe standing at the back.

The funeral of the Great Lafayette. The cortège can be seen entering Piershill Cemetery in Edinburgh. Thousands of people turned up to pay their respects.

the body was taken to Glasgow in preparation of the funeral. Three days later, a workman sifting through the rubble found a severed papier-mâché hand which pointed to the spot where an overlooked body lay. The body, adorned with rings, was later identified as Lafayette.

The funeral of the Great Lafayette took place on Sunday, 14 May. Houdini sent a wreath in the shape of the head of his dog, Beauty. The event was covered in the *Fife Free Press and Kirkcaldy Guardian* of Saturday, 20 May 1911:

The funeral of the chief victim of the Edinburgh Empire Theatre disaster, Sigmund Neuburger, known throughout the music-hall world as 'The Great

Lafayette' took place on Sunday afternoon to Piershill Cemetery, Edinburgh, in the eastern side of the city. The terrible nature of the disaster with its toll of human life, the mysterious personality of the dead illusionist with that compound of Oriental fatalism which showed itself in his actings prior to the occurrence, and the extraordinary turn of events whereby even in death and cremation illusion should linger, all went to provide elements that invested the funeral rites with peculiar interest. Huge crowds lined the route from Morrison Street to the cemetery, a distance of over two miles and the ordinary car and vehicular traffic was suspended.

The urn containing the remains of the 'Man of Mystery' was a massive oak urn, with a raised three-tier canopy lid. It bore the following inscription on a silver plate: 'The Great Lafayette, who perished in the Empire Palace fire, May 9, 1911.' The urn was lined with lead inside, hermetically sealed. After being deposited in the funeral car, a purple velvet pall on which was worked a white silk cross, hid it from view. It was in keeping with the express desire of the illusionist that the casket containing his ashes should be laid in the vault beside that of his favourite dog 'Beauty', and great care was taken in the selection of the urn that it should conform to a size that would best meet his expressed wish, and by its position indicate the sense of comradeship that had existed between the dog and his master during life.

The four-horsed car containing the casket with Lafayette's ashes was preceded by the members of Lafayette's company walking bareheaded as it approached the pathway leading to the summit of the mound.

Only about thirty people were present to witness the actual interment of the ashes in the casket containing the embalmed body of 'Beauty', these included Mr Neuburger (the brother of Lafayette), Mr Sam Lloyd, Mr Nesbit Bailie Smith Elliot, Councillor Boyd, the representatives of the Jewish community and the deceased's more intimate friends. The casket containing the ashes of the 'man of mystery' was enclosed in that containing the embalmed body of Lafayette's favourite dog 'Beauty', and was placed, as was directed by Lafayette himself, between the fore and the hind paws of the dog, the body of which lies on its side, with open eyes. To be so interred was the master magician's last wish. As the ashes were so laid, the band played the hymn, 'Days and moments quickly flying.'

The Reverend D Finlay Clark officiated at the graveside and he read a short allocution bearing upon the sad occasion and containing references to the final resurrection of the dead. He also offered up appropriate prayer and this being ended, the casket containing the ashes of Lafayette and the embalmed body of 'Beauty' were slowly lowered into the vault.

Altogether the wreaths numbered over 50. Two or three were very elaborately designed. Mdlle Lalla Selbini, who took the principal lady's part

The floral tributes to the Great Lafayette. Houdini sent a display in the shape of Lafayette's dog, Beauty.

in Lafayette's sketches, and took part in the act 'The Lion's Bride,' sent a beautiful floral representation of the proscenium orchestra and drop-screen of a theatre, the whole standing 6ft high by 4ft broad. Picked out in forget-me-nots on the background which formed the drop curtain were the words, 'The Last Act.'

One of the most remarkable was that sent by Houdini, the 'Handcuff King'. It represented the dog, 'Beauty', to which Lafayette was so devotedly attached, a framework of wire and moss being filled in with forget-me-nots. Thousands of flowers had been used in its composition. The inscription read – 'To the memory of my friend, from the friend who gave him his best friend, 'Beauty'. Mr Martin Harvey's tribute was a plain laurel wreath and there were wreaths also from Mrs and Miss Martin Harvey.

Many other wonderful and ornate wreaths were laid.

Meanwhile, ten thousand people witnessed the funeral at Sheffield of the two midgets who lost their lives with Lafayette in the Edinburgh Empire fire. Mounted policemen had to keep the way clear for the procession. A woman was knocked down by a car and seriously injured. The estate of the Great Lafayette was estimated to amount to over 100,000 pounds sterling.

On Friday, 19 May, the surviving members of Lafayette's troupe met at the Coliseum in London and decided that 'the show must go on'. It was reported that they had received many tempting offers to perform the show that they had rehearsed but it seemed that without Lafayette the show didn't have the same appeal. Lalla Selbini continued performing Lafayette's act 'The Lion's Bride' and toured theatres within Britain during 1912. She played to packed houses nightly.

Lafayette was said to have treated his company very well and paid them over the going rate. However, fellow magician Will Goldston wrote in his book, *Sensational Tales of Mystery Men*, that 'Lafayette was the most hated magician that ever lived. This is strange when one recalls that it was he who established the first class illusionist as an artist worthy of a high salary. He proved to the management of the Holborn Empire that he was worth every penny of the £500 a week he demanded, by taking over the theatre himself for a fortnight, and running it at a huge profit.

He was unsociable to a point of rudeness, and it was for this reason that he was universally disliked. His constant refusals to meet his brother conjurers, both here and in America, made him so intensely unpopular that he was greeted everywhere with the most utter and open contempt.'

Perhaps the description was unfair and it appeared that Lafayette would have rather had the company of his dog, Beauty, than that of his fellow magicians. Houdini, who was also friends with Goldin, must have thought something of him to give him the dog in the first place and to send such an elaborate and personal wreath to his funeral.

After the funeral of Lafayette, an argument arose over who should pay for the funeral service. The dispute continued for the next two years and was dragged through the courts. Lafayette's estate had been handed over to his sole next-of-kin, his brother Alfred, although creditors had been left unpaid. He argued that he shouldn't have to pay for the Great Lafayette's funeral, the funeral of his dog, Beauty, or for the cremation costs of the man whose body had been cremated when it was mistaken for his brother's.

Five years after his death, in the *Manchester Courier* of Wednesday, 22 March 1916, there appeared a story under the headline 'Disappearance of Illusionist's brother.' Creditors continued to chase Lafayette's brother, Alfred, who it was said had disappeared with every penny he could lay his hands on. A total of £12,000 was owed to the estate.

Lafayette was one of the greatest showmen of all time but is mainly remembered for the tragic events which led to his untimely death.

Chapter Two

Chung Ling Soo

C hung Ling Soo was born William Ellsworth Robinson in April 1861 in Westchester County, New York. Both of his parents were of Scottish descent and settled in Manhattan. His father, James Robinson toured as part of Charley White's Minstrel Show. He specialised in hypnotism, ventriloquism, impersonations and magic tricks. He later showed his son how to perform magic tricks.

At the age of 14, William Robinson performed his first magic act and joined a vaudeville tour where he was billed as 'Robinson the Man of Mystery'. In 1887, under the name 'Achmed Ben Ali', he performed 'black art illusions'. For the first time, Robinson copied the act of another magician, Max Auzinger, who was German and who performed under the similar sounding name of 'Ben Ali Bey'.

William Ellsworth Robinson otherwise known as Chung Ling Soo.

In 1896, after performing with the likes of Harry Kellar and Alexander Herrmann, he decided to go it alone. Robinson heard about a challenge issued by Ching Ling Foo, a well-known Chinese magician, which offered a prize of $1,000 to anyone who could copy his illusions. Robinson had watched Foo's act when he toured America and had worked out many of his illusions and decided to claim the $1,000. However, Foo refused to meet him because Robinson had responded to a previous challenge and lost. Robinson was upset by this dismissal.

By 1900, an agent was looking for a Chinese magician to appear at the Folies Bergère in Paris. Robinson accepted the job and started dressing in Chinese costume. He shaved his hair off and painted his face with greasepaint so as to appear darker. He copied much of Ching Ling Foo's act and started calling himself

'Hop Sing Soo'. He proved very popular and, by the time he reached the London stage, he was being billed as Chung Ling Soo. Robinson now claimed to be Chinese and his audience was fooled. He never spoke on stage, claiming he knew no English, and used an interpreter to speak to reporters. His assistant, and wife, on stage, Suee Seen (White Lily), also claimed to be Chinese but was born Olive Path, in America. She was very small in stature, standing at just 4ft 10in.

On Monday, 16 April 1900, Chung Ling Soo made his first appearance in Great Britain at the Alhambra in London. His act was mentioned in the *St James's Gazette* of Tuesday, 17 April 1900:

Chung Ling Soo in Chinese costume.

By way of an Easter novelty, Mr Dundas Slater has specially engaged the Chung Ling Soo company of Chinese magicians. These made their first appearance last night at the Alhambra, which, it may be mentioned, is their first appearance in Europe. Some of the smart tricks performed were decidedly novel, as, for instance, where the senior member of the company angles for fish in the air with a long rod, and as a result produces gold fish galore on his hook. Another trick by a young performer was the whirling round into all sorts of fantastic shapes and evolutions with two flaring torches at the end of a long chain. There is no doubt that our friend John Chinaman will be a highly popular part of the Easter programme at this place. The ballet, 'Soldiers of the Queen', is a finished patriotic and popular item.

A photo of Chung Ling Soo and his wife, Suee Seen, in their elaborate stage costumes.

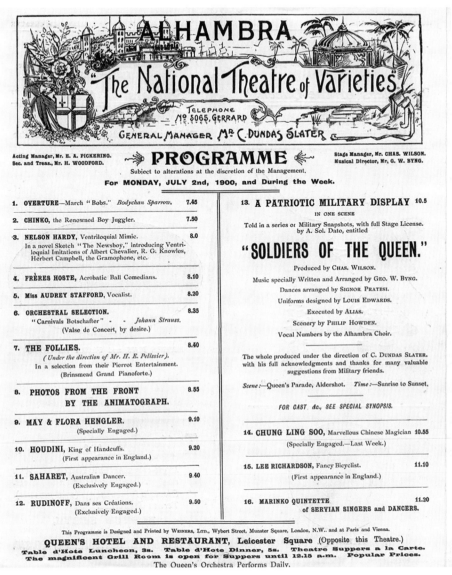

A programme for the Alhambra Theatre for July 1900. On the bill were Chung Ling Soo and Harry Houdini.

Chung Ling Soo appeared at the Alhambra Theatre until July 1900. Also on the bill in July was Harry Houdini who was making his first appearance in Great Britain.

An advert appeared in the *London and Provincial Entr'acte* which read: 'Warning. The conjuring performance of Chung Ling Soo, Chinese magician, now nightly presented at the Alhambra Theatre is protected by patents in England, France and

Germany through the agency of Raynor and Co, 37 Chancery Lane. Any infringement will be prosecuted.'

Chung Ling Soo was advertised at the Alhambra as being aided by his son and a Chinese maid 'in a most astonishing exhibition of legerdemain'.

As Chung Ling Soo, Robinson became hugely popular and was very soon one of the highest earners on the music hall circuit.

Of course, none of this pleased Ching Ling Foo, who had had his whole act stolen. While Soo was appearing at the London Hippodrome in January 1905, Foo was appearing at the nearby Empire Theatre. Foo knew that Chung Ling Soo was really an American called William Robinson and did his best to publicly expose Soo as an impostor. Foo issued Chung Ling Soo with a challenge saying that he would duplicate

A portrait of William Ellsworth Robinson as Chung Ling Soo, complete with pigtail.

A theatre poster advertising the illusions of Chung Ling Soo.

A theatre poster featuring Chung Ling Soo and Suee Seen.

Soo's act. They were to meet at the offices of the *Weekly Dispatch* but when Foo realised that the newspaper wasn't interested in exposing Soo as an American, he refused to show. This proved to be a public embarrassment for Foo who only played four weeks at the Empire while Soo's show continued for six months.

The *London Daily News* carried a photo of Chung Ling Soo and Suee Seen's three-year old daughter, Bamboo Leaf. It was clear from the photo that she wasn't the daughter of Chinese parents but Soo's deception was never questioned.

The *Burnley News* of Saturday, 6 November 1915 carried the story of Soo's forthcoming appearance in the city:

> Next week, the stage of the Empire will be transformed into a veritable palace of Aladdin, presided over by the greatest exponent of Eastern magic, Chung Ling Soo. This wonderful Chinaman will present a series of illusions which will realise in their oriental splendour and magnificence those mystifying features so closely associated with the Arabian Nights entertainments. A magician of international renown, this much travelled Chinaman with the assistance of a staff of celestials, headed by Miss Suee Seen, will present an entertainment identical in every respect to that which has bewildered vast audiences in all the great capitals of Europe, at present so prominent in the theatre of war.

A portrait shot of Chung Ling Soo which appeared in the *Derbyshire Courier* of May 1914.

Bamboo Leaf, the three-year-old daughter of Chung Ling Soo and Suee Seen as featured in the *London Daily News* of Thursday, 22 November 1906.

A portrait shot of Chung Ling Soo.

The performance will be divided into three parts at each house, the first portion consisting of a series of baffling acts of mysticism, presented in a gorgeous Eastern setting, followed in quick succession by an exposition of oriental illusions which have been invented by the great conjuror after years of study spent among the Llamas of Tibet and the remote cities of China and the Far East.

The entertainment will conclude with a grand patriotic spectacle entitled the 'World and its people' in which Chung Ling Soo will introduce a globe of the world and from which, with a wave of his fan, he will produce a procession of soldiers of the allied forces, concluding with a tableau realising Britannia's realm presented in a scene of dazzling splendour. On Saturday afternoon at 2.30, a matinee will be given when the Chinaman will give the entire entertainment lasting over two and a half hours, and will present a series of over fifty illusions. Chung Ling Soo will be supported by a strong variety company at each performance, with the exception of the matinee, when the great illusionist will be responsible for the whole programme.

Soo's most famous illusion was called 'Condemned to death by the boxers', where he caught a bullet in his teeth. This proved to be his downfall. On 23 March 1918, he was accidentally shot on stage at the Wood Green Empire in London while performing the trick. To keep up the deception that he was Chinese, he had never spoken on stage but, injured, uttered the words, 'Oh my God. Something's happened. Lower the curtain!' when he was shot. He was taken to hospital but died the next day. The story was carried in newspapers up and down the country.

An advert for a grand benefit matinee in aid of the Walsall and District Hospital on Saturday, 4 December 1909. The show featured Chung Ling Soo as well as many popular music hall acts of the day.

The first ladies night at the Magicians' Club in April 1913. Pictured are Harry Houdini (the chairman), Horace Goldin, Will Goldston, Chung Ling Soo, Harry Day, Stanley Collins, Jules Inger, W.C. Zelka and Bennett Scott as well as other members of the club.

The *Coventry Evening Telegraph* of Monday, 25 March 1918 reported:

> Chung Ling Soo, the well-known Chinese magician, who, however, was not a Chinaman, was fatally shot during his performance at the Wood Green Empire on Saturday night. The accident occurred at the second house and in connection with the final trick of the evening. Chung Ling Soo was taken to the Wood Green Hospital, where he lived only a few hours.
>
> Mr F Kametaro, stage manager to Soo for 16 years, stated last night: 'I was on the stage with two other assistants at the time. They both had guns and we called for a committee from the audience as usual. Two soldiers came up and

A group photo of Chung Ling Soo, Suee Seen and Bamboo Leaf. Their daughter obviously wasn't Chinese but this wasn't questioned.

examined the bullets put into the rifles and the powder. I directed them to go into a corner out of the way, and upon receiving the cue from Mr Soo, I gave the order to fire. Mr Soo had a china plate with which he was supposed to deflect the bullets. Both assistants fired and a gentleman in the audience stood up and said something to Mr Soo. When the second order was given, the gentleman stood up again. Mr Soo had been doing the trick for nine years. He always fixed the guns in his private room. After the bullets were fired, Mr Soo usually staggered and when he fell, I thought it was the usual performance. He then called out, "Oh, my God!" Upon going to him, we found that the bullet had passed right through him.'

It is understood the deception in the trick was that the bullets placed in the guns do not leave the muzzles but, by a device in the mechanism, remained in the gun. Why, on this occasion, the bullet was projected, is not at present known.

Mr Soo, who was an American, was 56 years old and had performed before the king on several occasions.

Private S Land, of the RFC, home on leave, who was present in the audience, said that as soon as the rifles were fired, Mr Soo fell down and at first the audience thought that it was part of the performance. Then the curtain was rung down and some pictures put on the screen and it became known that an accident had befallen the performer.

Ironically, the name Chung Ling Soo translated to 'Jolly Good Luck.' He became the thirteenth person to be tragically killed while performing the bullet trick and the stunt was later shunned by magicians.

For eighteen years, Chung Ling Soo had performed one of the most intriguing and interesting acts on the British stage. The fact that he wasn't actually Chinese and that he died while performing on stage has made him far more memorable than his adversary Ching Ling Foo, who is largely forgotten.

After his death, his widow, Suee Seen, kept the company together and toured as 'The Mysteries of Chung Ling Soo' during the rest of 1918. What happened to Suee Seen afterwards is a mystery. For a while she lived at Tennyson Place in Bradford and, from a letter she sent to *The Stage*, was still there in 1920. Some say that she returned to America with Houdini in 1920 while there are reports that she ran a shop in Bradford and was killed when the shop was destroyed by bombing in 1940.

Chapter Three

Datas

Datas wasn't an illusionist but his act performed with the best of them including Houdini and is worth mentioning because of his incredible ability to retain facts.

Datas was born William James Maurice Bottle in Newnham, in Kent on 20 July, 1875. His father worked as a cobbler. Bottle was unwell in his early years making him unable to walk until the age of 6. He came from a large family and, because of his illness, had received little schooling but learned to read and write and, by the age of 11, had found a job as a newspaper boy.

While still a boy, he worked for the South Eastern Railway and later as a van boy for the London Parcels Delivery Company. At the age of 16, he started work at the Crystal Palace Gas Works. He worked his way up to being a striker in the blacksmith's shop where he was paid twenty-four shillings a week. A chance meeting resulted in him leaving the gas works in June 1901 and embarking on a career in show business.

While taking a walk, he overheard two men talking about the date of the end of the great Tichborne trial. Neither of them knew the right date, so he interrupted and said: 'I beg your pardon, gentlemen, but the date of the close of the Tichborne trial was February 28th, 1874.' One of the gentlemen looked at him and commented, 'Why that was before you were born!' He replied, 'I am quite aware of that' before giving them all the important information featured in the famous trial. Datas saw this as his first public performance.

Discovering how surprised they were at his great store of knowledge, he continued with a number of dates of events in English history, together with the names of Derby and Oaks winners, all in rapid succession. A third man watched and was listening to the fascinating conversation. He approached Bottle and asked him, 'Would you like to go upon the stage?' Bottle thought that the man was joking, but he then slipped a sovereign into his hand and said, 'Come along with me and I will show you whether or not I am joking.'

Bottle was then led to the Standard Music Hall, Victoria, where he was asked to repeat his memory act. His popularity grew and at the end of an engagement of twelve months at the Palace Theatre, Shaftesbury Avenue, London, he was offered a twenty-week tour of Great Britain by Mr. H. E. Moss. He appeared at Glasgow, Edinburgh, Dublin, Liverpool, Birmingham and Sheffield, and during the tour many unusual questions were put to him all of which he answered instantly.

The *Era* of Saturday, 6 September 1902 called him the 'eighth wonder of the world'. The newspaper reported:

> It was Charles Morton, the genial manager of the Palace, who christened Datas 'The Living Encyclopaedia and Eighth Wonder of the World', and not without cause. He has dates and facts at his fingers' ends sufficient to confuse the greatest dominie in the world and many dons would be amazed at the rapid replies he gives to the most difficult conundrums in history, geography and other subjects. He makes a speciality of disasters, and calamities and great trials. Of course, there have been 'memorisers' on the music hall stage from the very beginning but up to the present, none has been half so wonderful as Datas.

A younger portrait of Datas featured in the *Era* of Saturday, 6 September 1902.

Datas's popularity in the theatre grew with people turning up to ask him all sorts of questions including the winners of forthcoming horse races. Datas liked a joke and always had a reply for any smart alec in the audience. His success led to him being offered work in America and Australia. Eventually, he toured Australia twice, New Zealand, South Africa, Tasmania, Ceylon, Johannesburg, America, Gibraltar and Naples. His catchphrase 'Am I right, Sir?' in answer to questions became well-known.

In an interview in 1902, Datas said:

> I am the son of a shoemaker and was born in Kent twenty-six years ago. I did not have much schooling; just enough to enable me to read and write – oh, I am always trying to learn and improve myself. At the age of fifteen, I got a job as a stoker at the Crystal Palace Gasworks and there I stoked for ten years until one afternoon a certain comedian overheard me and my mates discussing dates. He came up and spoke to me, with the result that I put my last scoop of coals in the retort at ten minutes to two on Monday afternoon, July 29th, 1901. I may say, however, I had one small engagement prior to the real beginning of my date career and I even offered myself to a certain London manager at a ridiculous sum. Well, so anxious was I to get on, that

that manager could have had me in the early days, before I threw up stoking, for a pound a week. He did not believe in 'memory matters'. I expect he has a memory of his own though now.

The *Sporting Times* of Saturday, 28 November 1903 mentioned banter between Datas and a member of his audience:

Datas, nee Mr. Bottle, has a way of his own of getting out of a tight place.
    'With whom did Jem Mace have his first fight in London?' somebody shouted.
    'It is not recorded—authorities differ,' answered Datas.

An advert from the *London and Provincial Entr'acte* of Saturday, 27 February 1904 announcing future shows from 'Morton's Man of Memory.'

An advert for Datas's show at the Palace Theatre in London during October 1904.

A muscular old 'un, with a battered proboscis, arose in his seat – it was Mace himself.

'It was with Bill Thorp,' cried Jem, 'a costermonger in South London.'

'Yes, yes, that's right,' dallied Datas, playfully, 'but there were two or three scraps in side streets before that, Mr. Mace!'

And the old 'un chuckled, but didn't deny it.

A macabre article appeared in the *Western Times* of Tuesday, 29 March 1904. It read:

Charles Peace, the well-known Victorian criminal, whose brain was almost as heavy as that of Datas.

Houdini, the man who cannot be manacled, and Datas, the man whose memory is almost infallible, must each of them have some faculty abnormally developed. The man who does not forget has already caught the eye of the medical faculty. He has received £2,000 on the understanding that on death his head shall be handed over to a famous London hospital.

Datas later wrote about how he came to sell his head:

It was on the occasion of my first trip to the States in 1904 when the papers had come out with the full history of the stoker with the phenomenal brain, that I sold my head. Naturally I was the subject of much medical speculation, and accordingly I was invited by four well-known American doctors to submit myself for examination. I was young, full of ambition, and not averse to the publicity which such an examination was bound to bring. The doctors were named Bailey, Crawford, Osian, and Carlton Senior, and I duly presented myself to them on behalf of the institution which they represented. They made all sorts of tests and eventually informed me that I had the heaviest brain of any man in the world. They measured and weighed it by various calculations, and informed me that my brain weighed 68 ounces, and that the heaviest brain before me was that of Couvier, which weighed 67 ounces, against that of Napoleon which weighed 66½ ounces. I did not tell them that the brain of Charles Peace, one of the most infamous criminals of all time, weighed 66 ounces. A tremendous brain which, had it been used for good purposes, might have gained for him a place amongst the greatest geniuses of all time instead of a prominent position in the rogues gallery. These four doctors were extremely interested in my head, and in the end they offered to buy it. I guess there are not many men who have sold their heads, and certainly very few who have been able to raise as much as £2,000 on it anyway. Well, that is the price for which I sold my head to these four doctors, £2,000 cash down. My ambition had not affected my commercial instincts you will observe. The agreement was duly drawn up and I parted with my head, only after my death, I must add. Of course, great publicity attached to this event, and

A portrait shot of Datas.

there were columns in the newspapers when the deal was finally through. I received my £2,000, and, here comes the ironic part, I have outlived all four of those doctors, who have thus been robbed of an interesting 'specimen', for I suppose that is how they looked upon me; whilst I have lived to enjoy that £2,000 to the full.

A comical true tale was told about Houdini and Datas. One night Datas approached Houdini stating that he had digs in the city but couldn't remember where they were. Houdini consoled him and invited him back to his lodgings but found that his landlady was out and he didn't have a key so couldn't get in. The irony was that Datas, the Memory Man, had forgotten where he was staying and Houdini, the king of locks, was unable to break in.

During 1905, Datas held the record engagement at the Palace Theatre, Richmond, playing for fifty-two continuous weeks.

During the First World War, Datas served time as a special constable.

Data had a fascination with crime and was friends with hangmen including James Berry, whose regular job was running a tobacco shop. He also associated with William Billington who had previously been a Sunday School teacher before becoming a hangman. Most of these associates Data met when they came to see his act. He was also friends with Dr Crippen and his wife, Cora, who Crippen was later found guilty of murdering. Another friend of Datas's was Jim Kelly, the younger brother of Ned Kelly. Jim Kelly and Data had travelled together across Australia with Wirth's Circus. Jim Kelly was the ringmaster.

Datas wrote in his biography:

From Jim, I heard many wonderful stories of his notorious brothers at first hand, and thus I am able to reveal much of the history of these outlaws who created a reign of terror amongst bank managers and mail coach drivers in Australia, and tell intimate stories of them which have hitherto never been told. Indeed, I always made a point of getting first-hand information about any date or incident I wished to memorise, as by that means I found that the event became more definitely fixed in my mind. I thus get a picture in my eye and whenever an event is mentioned, the picture rises up before me and the date follows automatically.

Datas's association with criminals and their executioners arose as he gathered more facts to include in his acts. It was quite common for questions to be asked from members of the audience about notorious and grizzly crimes.

A story of the infamous Babbacombe murder was featured in the *Western Times* of Tuesday, 8 April 1919. It read:

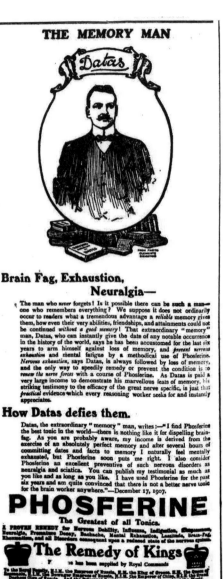

An advert for Phosferine endorsed by Datas for 'Brain Fog' and exhaustion as featured in the *Yorkshire Evening Post* of Thursday, 6 February 1908.

A rather interesting echo of the Babbacombe murder is provided in the *Daily Express*, obtained in the course of an interview with Datas, the memory man, who is well-known in Exeter. John Lee, as is well-known, was sentenced to death for murder and at Exeter prison, James Berry, the executioner, tried three times without success to hang him. Lee was released from prison some years ago. The *Daily Express* says: 'Datas, by the way, was the third person present at a

Morton's Man of Memory.
DATAS,
the Most Marvellous Man on Earth.
The Only Artist who ever Played Twelve Months right off at the Palace, Shaftesbury Avenue.
Monday, PALACE, DERBY.

An advert from March 1905 announcing Datas's appearance at the Palace, Derby.

friendly dinner which was enjoyed by John Lee, the Babbacombe murderer, and the late James Berry, the executioner, who tried to hang Lee three times but failed.'

The executioner and the man he could not hang met, through Datas' instrumentality, after Lee was released from penal servitude, and had exchanged reminiscences over a joint of mutton without the least suggestion of wounded professional pride on the one side or disappointment on the other.

'Berry, after ceasing to be an executioner, set up at Bradford as a phrenologist and character reader,' said Datas. 'His card bore the words, "Heads examined." He examined a good many heads in his time.'

In 1935, Alfred Hitchcock based the character 'Mr Memory,' in *The 39 Steps*, on Datas.

Datas was still touring theatres around Great Britain during the Second World War. He died in 1956 and, although it was previously promised to a London hospital, it's uncertain what happened to his brain.

Chapter Four

The Davenport Brothers

Ira Erastus Davenport (September 17, 1839–July 8, 1911) and William Henry Davenport (February 1, 1841–July 1, 1877) were American magicians who were better known as the 'Davenport Brothers'. They were born in Buffalo, the sons of a policeman. They began their act in 1854, a decade after spiritualism had taken off in America, and soon cashed in on the new religion. They were joined by William Fay, a conjurer, also from Buffalo. Their illusions claimed to show spirits from another world. Their show was introduced by Dr J.B. Ferguson, a former restoration movement minister. Ferguson believed that the Davenports had spiritual powers and could contact the dead.

The Davenport Brothers with William Fay, seated.

Their most famous illusion saw them tied up in a box which contained musical instruments. As soon as the box was closed, the instruments would play. When the door of the box was opened, the Davenports still had their hands bound.

They toured America for ten years with their act before heading towards England. Their spirit cabinet was investigated by the 'Ghost Club', a paranormal

An early advert for the Davenport Brothers shown taking part in Professor W.M. Fay's 'Dark Séance'.

PROF. W. M. FAY'S DARK SÉANCE.

investigation organisation set up in 1862. Their findings were never made public.

Far from being fooled, many of the general public were sceptical.

The *Brighton Gazette* of Thursday, 22 December 1864 reported:

We paid a visit to the 'séance' of the Davenport Brothers on Tuesday. We have for years heard of table-turning and table-rapping as holding sway in America but it is only of recent date that practical John Bull has regarded such matters with any other feeling than that of utter disgust. And now, the way being paved by certain itinerant

An early sketch showing the Davenport Brothers in their spirit cabinet surrounded by musical instruments.

lecturers – John Bull is found an easy gull for the hocus-pocus montebank performances of certain Yankees, whose feats of legerdemain – regarded strictly as such, pale before the really superior displays of Anderson, Frikell, Jacobs or a score of other so-called 'wizards' of east, west, north or south but whose 'performances' are sought off to be palmed off upon us by clap-trap and an assumption of science.

We give the 'showman' of the Davenports – we beg pardon – the 'Rev' Dr Ferguson, credit for cleverly introducing his 'entertainment' by disclaiming all attempt to herald it as either material or spiritualistic – that he says he leaves to each one's convictions. But what shall we say of Mr Cooper, of Eastbourne, who, in a short address, opens this 'performance'? We thought we had heard the last of this gentleman, when, on a recent visit to Brighton, in maintaining his theory of spiritualism, he met with formidable opponents at our Town Hall; but to our sorrow we find him now coming forward producing this juggle as an 'ocular demonstration of facts', and contending that all that is presented is the work of 'Spirits, good and bad, who return from the spirit world!'

Of the performance, we have little to say: we were disappointed in it; it was contemptible and many were the long faces drawn at its conclusion in regret of money thrown away – paid for admission. After this precaution, if our readers will be 'taken in', on themselves be the blame. One amusing circumstance, we must relate. The 'showman' – no, the 'Rev', in true conjuror's style, proposed doing the flour trick, a trick the merit of which consists in the 'Brothers' hands being filled with flour, they then being tied and enclosed, whilst, in the semi-darkness, hands appear at the opening of the cabinet. Mr Malden, of Windlesham House, who was seated in the front row of the stalls, being anxious to see this test properly made, went on the platform and, in answer to the showman's request, told the audience that flour had been deposited in the performer's hands, 'about a teaspoonful'. 'Quite sufficient for all practical purposes,' said the showman – the trick was performed and the assertion made that no flour had been spilled, hence the inference that the 'Brothers' had no hand in the 'trick'. Mr Malden examined the carpet on the floor of the cabinet and, holding it up to the eyes of the audience, exhibited slight but unmistakable traces of flour thereupon. 'Oh the quantity is so very trifling,' said the showman but Mr Malden's answer was so apropos, 'Quite sufficient for all practical purposes.' Hearty applause and roars of laughter succeeded and, somewhat discomforted, Mr Showman pronounced the entertainment at an end, amidst the ridicule and contempt of the major part of the audience.

On Wednesday, 15 February 1865, the Davenports appeared at St George's Hall, Liverpool and asked for members of the audience to tie the brothers up before they entered their cabinet. The audience members, Mr Cummings and Mr Hulley, tied their hands but used special knots so that the Davenports couldn't escape. Realising this, Ira Davenport called for Dr Ferguson to cut him free. Ira showed blood on the back of his hand saying the cut was caused by his tying up but this wasn't the case. He knew that if he was tied this way that he wouldn't be able to escape in the cabinet to play the instruments therein. The Davenports stormed off the stage. Realising that the whole act was a sham, the audience rioted and went on stage and smashed up the Davenports' cabinet. Three to four hundred people from the audience then marched to Union Hotel in Clayton Square where the Davenports were staying to demand their money back. This was refused. A court action was later taken by Mr Cummings which resulted in everybody's money being refunded.

John Nevil Maskelyne, a stage magician, had already realised how the cabinet illusion was performed and proceeded to expose the trick. He revealed all, with his own specially-built cabinet, to an audience during a show at Cheltenham in June 1865. Other magicians, including Jean Eugene Robert-Houdin and John Henry Anderson, wrote exposés of the Davenport Brothers and performed identical tricks. A pair of amateur magicians followed the Davenports on their tours and tied them with knots that were difficult to escape from. The illusion failed and audiences again asked for their money back.

An early photograph of the Davenport Brothers in their mystical cabinet.

Bell's Weekly Messenger of Saturday, 12 November 1870 reported:

The Davenport Brothers who assume to have spiritual aid in giving their exhibitions, were lately detected in their tricks and publicly exposed at Ray City, Michigan. The Brothers claim that the hands that present themselves from the orifice are spiritual and not flesh and blood. When the 'spiritual

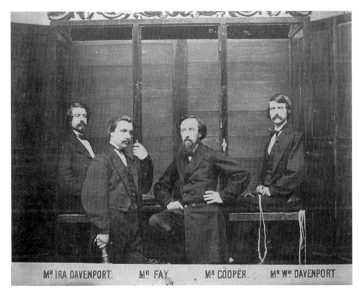

MR IRA DAVENPORT.   MR FAY.   MR COOPER.   MR WM DAVENPORT.

Ira Davenport, William Fay, Mr Cooper and William Davenport.

hand' made its appearance, a gentleman on the platform seized it and besmeared it with printers' ink, which nothing short of oil or some alkali will remove. When the brothers came forth into the light they were marked men, the printers' ink still remaining upon their hands. They were received with hisses and groans, after which the audience dispersed.

William Henry Davenport died in 1877 bringing the act to an end. Ira Erastus rejoined William Fay in 1896 and toured across America but their act wasn't successful. Ira died in 1911.

While appearing at the Empire in Sheffield in March 1920, Harry Houdini sent Sir Arthur Conan Doyle a copy of his book, *The Unmasking of Robert-Houdin* to which Conan Doyle had shown great interest particularly in a section which mentioned the Davenport Brothers. Conan Doyle was a devout spiritualist and believed in the work of mediums while Houdini realised that all the results were achieved by trickery.

While appearing at the Empire in Sheffield, Houdini wrote a letter to Conan Doyle which read :

Empire, Sheffield
17.3.20

Dear Sir Arthur Conan Doyle:

Pleased to hear from you and that you were interested about some of the points in my book.

Regarding the Davenport Brothers: It will interest you to know that I was an intimate friend of Ira Erastus Davenport, and was the last man outside his family circle to visit him in Maysville, Chautauqua County, New York. In fact he was waiting for me and passed away the morning I was leaving to pay him my annual visit.

I can make the positive assertion that the Davenport Brothers never were exposed. Their first trouble at the Salle Herz, in Paris, came about through the fact that one of the legs of the cabinet was dislodged, and the cabinet tripped over, and this happened only a short time after the arrival of the brothers in Paris.

The trouble they had in Leeds and Liverpool did not arise from the fact that they were exposed. Mr. Ira Davenport told me they were bound so inhumanely that Dr. Ferguson cut the rope before the séance started (in Liverpool).

I know for a positive fact that it was not essential for them to release these bonds in order to obtain manifestations.

The reason why Mr. Ira Davenport became so friendly with me was that, during my tour around the world, I visited the cemetery where his brother, William Henry Harrison was buried near Melbourne, Australia. His grave had not been visited for many years and I had it put in order.

I have all the Davenport Brothers' scrapbooks, and intend, some time in the future, to write a biography about their career from a different 'angle' than any which have hitherto appeared.

I trust you will not think I am egotistical in making this statement; that I know more about the Davenport Brothers than anyone living. The widow is still alive and there are two sons and a daughter in this 'vale of tears'.

I remember distinctly, in talking to Mr Davenport, that he was astonished at my knowledge of their tours, and he remarked, 'Houdini, you know more about myself than I do.'

Regarding my own work, I never claim spiritualistic or supernatural aid, always informing the public that it is accomplished by natural means, or as you suggest by 'art and practice'.

I don't want to write a long letter, so will close.

Sincerely yours,
Harry Houdini.

Conan Doyle later wrote to Houdini: 'I've been reading the Davenport book you gave me. How people could imagine those men were conjurers is beyond me.'

Conan Doyle believed whole-heartedly that the Davenports were genuine mediums but most realised that the act was just a clever illusion. Nevertheless, for a while they made a very good living from it.

Chapter Five

Ching Ling Foo

Ching Ling Foo was born in Beijing in China in 1854. His real name was Zhu Liankui. He was a well-respected entertainer in his own country but found fame in the UK during the early part of the 1900s. His stage act included breathing smoke and fire, producing a 15-foot-long pole from his mouth and the beheading of a serving boy. At the end of the performance, the boy, would return, unharmed, on to the stage.

Previously, in 1898, he had toured America. One of his tricks performed there was pulling a small boy out of a bowl of water. He offered anyone in the audience $1,000 if they could replicate the trick. As already mentioned, William Robinson, a part-time magician from New York, tried to claim the $1,000. Foo

Ching Ling Foo with his bowl of water illusion.

rebuffed him and Robinson took on the guise of Chung Ling Soo and travelled to Europe, posing as Chinese and stealing much of Foo's act.

By 1905, Foo was becoming well-known in Great Britain and his act drew thousands.

The *Leeds Mercury* of Monday, 2 January 1905 wrote about Ching Ling Foo and the abolition of the pigtail in China:

According to Ching Ling Foo, the Chinese juggler, pigtails will not be worn by Chinamen this year thanks to an edict issued by the Dowager Empress.

'They have been worn during the past three centuries as a sign of servitude to the ruling dynasty. I am glad they are about to be abolished because they are expensive and give a great deal of trouble.'

The Empress has also issued an edict prohibiting women's feet from being crushed but this is not so popular because the Chinese admire small-footed women.

The *London Daily News* of Wednesday, 4 January 1905 carried a story under the headline 'Ching Ling Foo at the Empire'. It read:

Ching Ling Foo, the original Chinese conjurer, about whom the public has read so much of late, has just made his first bow to an English audience at the Empire. His clever tricks left a deep impression upon the minds of those who saw him, and judging by the success that attended his initial appearance, the management knew what they were doing when they agreed to pay the performer a salary of £250 a week. Ching Ling Foo, who is described as the greatest living magician, claims to be the first Chinese conjurer to appear on any foreign stage. He is accompanied by his wife and a company of Chinese contortionists, acrobats and jugglers as well as his little daughter, Chee Ling, whose coon songs are one of the most interesting features of the show.

By 1905, Foo was performing at the London Empire. His rival Chung Ling Soo was performing at the nearby Hippodrome.

The *Dundee Evening Post* of Monday, 9 January 1905 reported:

Ching Ling Foo, who is appearing at the Empire Theatre, has sent out a challenge to Chung Ling Soo, who is engaged at the Hippodrome, to the effect that he will forfeit £1,000 if Chung Ling Soo succeeds in doing any of his twenty tricks. Today, the test as to which is the best magician will take place before an audience of journalists. Ching asserts that Chung is not a Chinaman but a Scottish American.

The challenge didn't go ahead and there were reports that Foo didn't turn up. This was said to have damaged his reputation and there are few reports of any other appearances in the UK for several years.

Foo apparently appeared in Hull before his London appearance and details of this appeared in the *Hull Daily Mail* of Tuesday, 10 January 1905. It's obvious, like many people of the time, the writer is confusing Foo and Soo and even claims that Foo is a native of Birmingham. The article read:

What with Ching and Chung, I am getting a little mixed up. The other week, Ching Ling Foo appeared at the Hull Palace of Varieties, just at the time that Chung Ling Soo was making his debut in London. Ching and Chung are conjurers both. I have seen Ching. They tell me he is a native of Birmingham. But I have not seen Chung, who, they assert is a genuine Chinaman. Two names so much alike, two men doing the same kind of trick – what more natural than that there should come forth mystery and rivalry and all manner of strange mixings. So a combat was arranged. Ching challenged Chung. The place was appointed, the hour was fixed and Chung the Chinaman turned up with his wonderful celestial retinue. But Chung, the Mandarin of the One Button, waited in vain for Ching. The longer Ching remained away, the broader grew the smile

An advert for Ching Ling Foo's show at the Empire during July 1914.

of Chung. 'Ha! Ha!' he laughed. He had done the impossible. He had made his rival invisible. And another impossible thing he did. Ching Ling Foo in his challenge, had promised to forfeit a thousand pounds if his rival Chung Ling Soo could perform ten of his Ching Ling Foo's twenty tricks. And, so it is said, in the presence of the invisible Ching Ling Foo, Chung Ling Soo executed ten of Ching Ling Foo's tricks – tricks we have seen him perform in his fortnight's stay in Hull. How did the invisible Ching feel as he, seeing but unseen, beheld his rival Chung accomplish his feat?

Between Foo's appearances in 1905, little is reported of him in British newspapers until 1914. It's known that after leaving the UK, he toured Germany. He was back in the UK in 1914 just before the outbreak of the First World War.

The *Daily Record* of Saturday, 4 July 1914 reported:

China's great magician and necromancer, Ching Ling Foo, will be at the Empire. Since his engagement in London, he has been touring Mongolia and North and South America, under the management of George and Leon Mooser of Shanghai. Ching Ling Foo, with his own company of Orientals, will come direct from China for this engagement.

An older Ching Ling Foo pictured with Harry Houdini.

He was billed as the 'World's Greatest Magician'. Also on the bill were his daughter, Chee Toy, Chinese Soubrette; Liu Chin Tang and his marvellous Diablo; and Li Lea Tseng, Wizard of the Whirling Spears.

Ching Ling Foo made his first appearance in Birmingham towards the end of July 1914.

The *Birmingham Daily Gazette* of Tuesday, 28 July 1914 wrote of Ching Ling Foo's appearance there:

> Mirth and mystery have leading exponents at the Empire this week. The versatility of Harry Weldon displayed in his burlesques moves everyone to unrestrained laughter. As the 'White hope', he will not get knocked out for a long time judging by the enthusiasm with which he was received last evening. The mystery is supplied by Ching Ling Foo, who produces bowls of water and other objects with the utmost facility but apparently from nowhere. He is supported by a numerous company who present an excellent programme, one of the best items being the pretty singing in English of Miss Chee Toy, a dainty little Chinese lady.

After Chung Ling Soo's death in 1918, many newspapers reported the rivalry between the two entertainers. Whereas the newspapers had previously sided with Soo, it seemed that they were now on the side of Foo.

The *Yorkshire Evening Post* of Monday, 25 March 1918 reported:

> Chung Ling Soo's tragic death on the stage recalls (the *London Evening News* says), one of the most audacious achievements of modern showmanship. For many years, the most popular entertainer in America was Ching Ling Foo, a genuine Chinese, of gentle birth, and wonderful skill. His earnings were fabulous.
>
> At one theatre, his success was in the balance when William Robertson, an American, arrived at the opposition theatre, calling himself Chung Ling Soo, challenged the other's good faith and aristocratic birth, and hounded him out of the city, claiming that he, Robertson, was the genuine Chinese of princely lineage. For a long time, he affected Chinese dress and manner of living and only conversed with English people during an interpreter. It was probably the first bluff since Barnum.

Ching Ling Foo died in China in 1922 but the circumstances surrounding his death remain a mystery. The Ching Ling Foo Company, led by Foo's daughter, Chee Toy, continued to tour well into the 1930s.

Chapter Six

Houdini

Harry Houdini was born Erik Weisz in Hungary on 24 March 1874. However, he claimed he was born in Appleton, Wisconsin on 6 April 1874. He was the son of Rabbi Mayer Samuel Weiss and his wife, Cecilia. He had a very close bond with his mother all his life.

Erik was one of seven children and had five brothers and one sister. One of his brothers, Herman, died at a young age.

On 3 July 1878, he travelled to the United States sailing on the SS *Fresia* with his mother and brothers and they settled in Appleton, Wisconsin where Erik's father served as a Rabbi. They changed the spelling of their surname to Weiss and Erik's name became Ehrich. His friends called him 'Ehrie' or 'Harry'.

At the age of 9, Ehrich gave his first public appearance when he performed as a trapeze artist and was billed as the 'Prince of the Air'. When Ehrich became a magician, he changed his name to Harry Houdini. The Houdini part of his name came from the French magician Jean Eugene Robert-Houdin, who he greatly admired.

Houdini started performing magic in 1891 and entertained with card tricks at sideshows and dime museums. At the time, he called himself 'The King of Cards'.

He later became interested in escape acts and appeared with his brother, Theo (Hardeen) who Houdini also called 'Dash'. In 1893, while performing at Coney Island with Theo, he met Wilhelmina Beatrice Rahner (Bess). Houdini married Bess and she replaced Theo in his act.

In 1899, Houdini met his future manager, Martin Beck in Woodstock, Illinois. Beck was

A photo of a young Harry Houdini in dress suit, handcuffs, leg irons and chains.

impressed by Houdini's stage act and booked him to appear on the Orpheum vaudeville circuit. In 1900, Beck arranged for Houdini to tour Europe. His first interviews in London were unsuccessful until he escaped from handcuffs at Scotland Yard baffling his captives. He was booked at the Alhambra Theatre for six months by its manager, C. Dundas Slater. So began a series of tours around Great Britain that would continue for the next twenty years.

The *London Evening Standard* of Tuesday, 3 July 1900 reported on the great success of Houdini's performance. It read:

> A novel feature in the programme at the Alhambra is the exhibition of skill by Mr Harry Houdini in releasing himself from handcuffs and other fetters. He made his first public appearance in London last night and his dexterity in escaping from handcuffs handed to him from the audience elicited the heartiest applause. Mr Houdini does not simply slip the shackles from his arms and legs but absolutely unlocks them without the aid of keys or springs. A member of the audience, who said that up to that time he had always claimed the title which had been given to Mr Houdini of 'King of Handcuffs,' placed a pair of these instruments on the wrists of the performer who speedily freed himself from their grip much to the astonishment of the owner. At the conclusion of the severe tests, Mr Houdini was recalled and applauded again and again.

The *London Evening Standard* of Tuesday, 10 July 1900, reported that two sailors of Her Majesty's ship *Powerful* had secured Houdini with a pair of ship's irons, placing him in what was called the cockfighting position with his arms on each side of his knees. His hands were locked in front of his legs and then a broom handle was inserted between his legs and arms so that he couldn't move. Houdini was lifted into a cabinet but was soon free. Several of his challenges over the next few years were remarkably similar leading to some suggesting that the trials were arranged by Houdini's entourage.

A publicity photo showing Houdini in chains and padlocks.

On Saturday, 21 July 1900, the *Era* reported:

A remarkable performance is that given by Houdini, who comes from America. He challenges anyone present to secure his wrists with handcuffs in such a manner that he cannot in a few minutes free himself. A committee of investigation is formed and on the night of our visit amongst the gentlemen who went on the stage was ex-Inspector Moore, of the Metropolitan Police, who, it was announced, has had eighteen years' experience in the handcuffing of criminals. Two pairs of handcuffs were placed on Houdini's wrists and were closely examined and thoroughly tested by the ex-police inspector and others. He then retired behind a screen and, at the expiration of a few minutes, reappeared having freed himself from the handcuffs. Again secured in a similar fashion but with his hands behind him, he liberated himself while facing the audience. Another astonishing trick is performed. Houdini, handcuffed as before, and wearing a coat belonging to one of the committeemen, envelopes himself in a sack which is securely tied and sealed. He is then placed in a strong box which is locked and corded. A few seconds and it is found that the young lady assistant has changed places with the prisoner and that she is wearing the borrowed coat.

By Saturday, 18 August 1900, the *Era* was reporting:

How Houdini, 'the king of handcuffs', manages to release himself from his iron bonds is inexplicable. Many experts in the 'darby' line go on the stage and endeavour to fetter Houdini with their appliances; but the result is always the same – the production of the handcuffs and the reappearance of the 'king' free and smiling. The variation on the well-known box trick with which Houdini concludes his show is decidedly neat and smart.

Houdini appeared in Great Britain many times over the next twenty years covering nearly all parts of the UK. Houdini became well-known as 'The Handcuff King' and as well as England, toured Scotland, the Netherlands, Germany, France, and Russia. While in Moscow, Houdini escaped from a Siberian prison transport van.

While performing on stage at the Hippodrome in 1904, Houdini was approached by a reporter from the *Daily Illustrated Mirror* who challenged him to escape from a specially-made pair of handcuffs. Houdini examined them and refused the challenge. 'These are not regulation handcuffs,' he said. The challenger motioned to the orchestra to stop playing, and when they did, he announced: 'On behalf of my newspaper, the *Daily Illustrated Mirror*, I have just challenged Mr Houdini to permit me to fasten these handcuffs on his wrists. Mr

Houdini declines. In the course of my journalistic duties this week, I interviewed a blacksmith at Birmingham named Nathaniel Hart who has spent five years of his life perfecting a lock, which he alleges no mortal man can pick. The handcuff I wish to fasten on Mr Houdini contains such a lock. The key alone took a week to make. The handcuffs are made of the finest British steel, by a British workman, and being the property of the *Daily Illustrated Mirror*, has been bought with British gold. Mr Houdini is evidently afraid of British-made handcuffs, for he will not put on this pair.'

Houdini repeated that they were not regulation handcuffs and, turning his back on the journalist, he allowed himself to be handcuffed by three other challengers. He escaped in minutes. The *Mirror* journalist asked Houdini if he could examine one of the pairs of handcuffs from which he'd just escaped. Houdini handed him a locked pair. The journalist banged the cuffs hard on the steps leading up to the stage. They sprang open much to the audience's amazement and delight. 'So much for regulation handcuffs!' the reporter shouted.

Once more he issued the challenge to Houdini. Houdini addressed the audience and said: 'I cannot possibly accept this gentleman's challenge tonight because I am restricted as to time. His handcuffs, he admits, have taken an artificer five years to make. I know, therefore, I can't get out of them in five minutes. There is not one lock in those handcuffs, but a half a dozen or more. I will make a match if the management here will allow me a matinee some day next week to make a trial. It will take me a long time to get out, even if I can do.'

The manager of the Hippodrome, Mr Parker, agreed to the event taking place on Thursday, 17 March 1904. Houdini wrote in his diary that London was in an uproar and that every paper was carrying the story. This was far better publicity than he could have hoped for and surpassed the interest gained by his usual jail breaks.

With all the publicity, over 4,000 people and 100 journalists turned up to witness the feat. The handcuffs were placed on Houdini and he disappeared behind a small screen to make his escape. Over an hour passed, with Houdini occasionally appearing from behind the screen still cuffed. At one point, he requested that the cuffs be taken off so that he could remove his coat. Frank Parker, the *Mirror*'s representative, refused saying that if the cuffs were to be removed, Houdini would be able to tell how they were undone. On hearing this, Houdini produced a penknife and, holding it with his teeth, proceeded to cut his coat off himself. At one point, after about fifty-six minutes, Houdini's wife came onto the stage to give him a kiss. Many believed later that the key to unlock the cuff was in her mouth. Houdini disappeared behind the screen and after an hour and ten minutes, he freed himself. The gathered crowd cheered and applauded him loudly and he was carried on their shoulders. He later wept saying that it had been the most difficult escape of his career.

It was suggested many years after his death that the whole performance had been staged between the *Daily Mirror* and Houdini and his difficulty escaping was just to add more suspense to the show. After the show, Houdini was presented with a sterling silver replica of the cuffs in honour of his escape. The miraculous act was reported in all newspapers throughout Britain. On 18 March, Houdini wrote in his diary: 'All English newspapers have wonderful accounts of me escaping out of *Mirror* handcuffs, greatest thing that any artist had in England. Extras were out and it was a case of nothing but "Houdini at the Hippodrome".'

Three days after the challenge was complete, Houdini offered a challenge to the *Mirror*. He told them, 'You challenged me, now I challenge the world!' He handed the newspaper a statement which read:

London Hippodrome, March 20, 1904.

To Whom it May Concern!

Since my success in mastering the celebrated *Daily Mirror* Handcuff it has come to my knowledge that certain disappointed, sceptical persons have made use of most unjust remarks against the results of last Thursday's contest. In particular, one person has had the brazen audacity to proclaim himself able to open the *Mirror* handcuff in two minutes. Such being the case, I hereby challenge any mortal being to open the *Mirror* Handcuff in the same space of time that I did. I will allow him the full use of both hands; also any instrument or instruments, barring the actual key. The cuff must not be broken or spoilt. Should he succeed, I will forfeit 100 guineas.

Harry Houdini.

Once published, Houdini received challenges from all over the country.

In 1906, Houdini, during his stage act, started to include movies of himself, performing amazing escapes and feats. By 1908, Houdini was performing the Milk Can Escape. It involved him being handcuffed and sealed inside a large galvanised milk can filled with water. The escape attracted huge audiences to his shows.

In 1909, Houdini bought a French Voisin biplane and made his first successful flight in Hamburg, Germany on 26 November. In 1910, he toured Australia and flew the plane there. He made three flights at Diggers Rest, near Melbourne on 18 March 1910, making him one of the earliest aviators in the country.

After returning from Australia, he put the plane into storage and never flew again.

Around 1912, he started to introduce the Chinese water torture cell into his act. His feet were locked in stocks before he was lowered upside down into a secure tank filled with water.

Another of his stunts included him being straitjacketed and hung upside down by his ankles by a crane or tall building. The outside performances attracted thousands of spectators and Houdini always successfully made his escape. Another outdoor publicity stunt involved him being secured in a packing case and lowered into the water. On 7 July 1912, he first performed the escape in New York's East River.

Houdini performing the vanishing elephant illusion at New York's Hippodrome Theater on 7 January 1918.

Houdini in handcuffs and leg manacles preparing for an escape from a submerged crate.

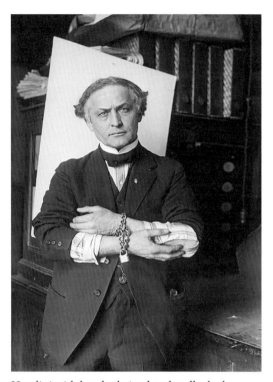

Houdini with hands chained and padlocked.

Houdini performing the Water Torture Cell stunt.

He first performed his Buried Alive stunt in Santa Ana, California in 1915. He almost died performing the feat after being buried in a pit six feet deep. He managed to claw his way to the surface but collapsed soon after.

In 1918, Houdini signed a contract to star in a serial called *The Master Mystery* which was shown in movie theatres around the world in 1919. He later went on to appear in *The Grim Game* (1919) and *Terror Island* (1920).

Houdini's six month tour of Great Britain in 1920 proved to be his most successful ever. When he left, he wouldn't have realised that this was to be his last tour of Britain. However, he now had other interests which included making movies and writing. By 1920, Houdini was spending a lot of his time debunking spiritualists who he believed to all be fakes. His friend, Sir Arthur Conan Doyle, believed totally in spiritualism and this eventually led to them falling out.

While appearing at the Princess Theatre in Montreal, Houdini was given several surprise blows to his abdomen by a McGill University student, J. Gordon Whitehead. The incident took place in Houdini's dressing room. Before punching him, Whitehead had asked Houdini if he believed in the miracles of the Bible and whether it was true that punches in the stomach did not hurt him. Houdini had been able to withstand similar blows but was completely unprepared for the attack. At the time, he was reclining on a couch after breaking his ankle several days earlier.

Houdini, although in great pain, continued to perform on stage and the discomfort lasted for a further two days before he finally saw a doctor. He had a high temperature and was found to have acute appendicitis. The doctor advised him that he needed an operation. Houdini, however, decided to carry on performing and took to the stage at the Garrick Theater in Detroit, Michigan, on 24 October 1926. He passed out during the show but recovered and carried on. Afterwards he was taken to Detroit's Grace Hospital. Houdini died several days later of peritonitis due to a ruptured appendix on 31 October 1926. The connection between the incident in the dressing room and his death was unclear. However, Houdini's insurance company took this as the cause of death.

Houdini was just 52 years old when he died and although he was nearing the end of his career, the world lost a great showman whose name would forever become synonymous with great feats of escape.

Chapter Seven

The Human Fly

Long before the *Marvel* comic superhero of the same name, the Human Fly scaled tall buildings, theatres and leapt from bridges. There were several performers who billed themselves as 'The Human Fly' and the death of one of the earliest was reported in the *Era* of Saturday, 19 September 1891: 'On Saturday, an inquest was held before Dr Moody, borough coroner, at the Prince of Wales' Theatre, Great Grimsby, on the body of Sydney Bird, known as Una, the human fly, who was killed by a fall while performing there on Friday night.'

Bird was the son of a gymnast and had been trained in the profession since 1884. His father stated in court that his son had performed the act for five years and had never had a mishap. There was no net when Bird fell from a height of 15ft and his father had tried to catch him but only caught his thumb in his jacket.

His father stated at the hearing:

> He was a very good boy. He very seldom tasted drink and had had none that day. The accident occurred between ten and eleven o'clock and when he fell upon the boards, I picked him up. He was quite insensible and only lived about two hours after the accident, lying unconscious the whole time.

Sydney Bird's funeral was attended by about 2,000 people.

There was another Human Fly in 1904, an act billed as 'Aric – The Human Fly' but little is recorded of his performance. Rodman Law carried the title during the early days of movies.

The *Nottingham Evening Post* of Saturday, 7 February 1914 reported:

CANTERBURY THEATRE
of VARIETIES.
Proprietors, Messrs. CROWDER and PAYNE.
Every Evening. Monster Programme of Unrivalled Attractions.—Production of BURMAH, by Harry Day, a grand Musical Military Entertainment, illustrating the life of a soldier, in three tableaux, England, India, and Burmah. Musical Mélange, "The Album of Beauties," introducing the renowned Mr. John D'Auban, Miss Emma D'Auban, and Company. The charming Sisters Leamar, Stebb and Trepp, Rowe and Athol, Brown, Newland, and Wallace; Cheevers and Kennedy, Grace Whiteford, Dan Leno, Frank Egerton, Thompson Trio, Henry Cardale, Harry Leander, &c. Open at 7.30; commence at 7.30. Side door, to avoid the crowd, open at 7 on Saturdays, 3d each extra. Prices, 6d to £2 2s.
Musical Director, Mr. E. BOSANQUET. Band Rehearsal Saturday and Monday at 1 o'clock sharp.
General Manager, Mr. A. THIODON.
LOOK OUT FOR THE HUMAN FLY.

An advert from the *London and Provincial Entr'acte* of Saturday, 3 July 1886 announcing the appearance of the Human Fly at the Canterbury Theatre of Varieties.

In the presence of thousands of spectators, Rodman Law, who describes himself as a 'sensation specialist,' ascended a tower of the Williamsburg Bridge, New York, which is almost as high as the Tower Bridge, London, and dived into the icy waters of the River Hudson. The object was to rescue a pretty blonde, Miss Constance Bennett, who had leapt from the bridge a few minutes before, with a parachute to regulate her flight.

Moving picture operators below the bridge reproduced in film every detail of the daring episode but women in the tramcars, who imagined that a dreadful tragedy was happening, shrieked and some fainted. The couple had evaded the police at the bridge and were at the summit of the tower before the police realised that they had been hoodwinked. In the river, a tug was waiting to rescue the man and woman with lifelines.

Harry Gardiner (the Human Fly) scaling the walls of the Camden New Jersey Courthouse on 10 February 1915.

Law first achieved notoriety as the 'human fly.' He climbed several of the loftiest skyscrapers in New York by crawling from coping to coping. His next feat was to enclose himself in a metal tube and to be blown from the mouth of a cannon. He narrowly escaped death because the tube cracked and Law was severely burned.

In 1923, Sir Arthur Conan Doyle wrote to Harry Houdini:

My dear Houdini:-
For goodness' sake take care of those dangerous stunts of yours. You have done enough of them. I speak because I have just read of the death of the 'Human Fly.'
Is it worth it?

Yours very sincerely,
A. CONAN DOYLE.'

Conan Doyle was referring to a different human fly, Howard Young. Reports of his death were carried in newspapers all around the world on 6 March 1923:

Hundreds of spectators in the streets were horrified yesterday, when Howard Young, who had obtained considerable note recently as 'the Human Fly,' fell eight storeys to his death, from the face of the Hotel Martinique, which he was trying to scale. It was understood that Young was performing for motion pictures and dozens of cameras were turned on him the moment he fell.

After the tragedy, yards of film were taken showing the action of the crowd. His wife was among those in the street watching him perform his daring feat and she fainted. Young was one of the organizers of the so-called Safety First Society, formed for the benefit of those engaged in occupations of more than ordinary danger.

A contract with a moving picture firm was found in the dead man's pocket. He wore white duck clothing, the better to set off his figure against the drab background of the buildings and across his shoulders, in large letters, were printed 'Safety First'.

In the same year as Young's death, Jack Lamonte was also being billed as the Human Fly. During April 1923, he scaled up the side of a post office in Quebec, Canada. It was stated that he had been doing stunts of this kind for seventeen years and during the First World War had been employed to raise funds for the Victory Loan campaign. In his career, he scaled some of the world's tallest buildings including the L.C. Smith building in Seattle, Washington, which was forty-two storeys high, as well as the Flat Iron building in New York which he climbed blindfolded. Lamonte was probably the best known 'human fly' but, today, is largely forgotten.

In December 1931, a cat burglar called George Bruce was sentenced to three months' hard labour. He was described as 'the cleverest cat burglar in England' and was known as the 'human fly' in America because of his agility. It is said that he mystified the police in America with his clever climbing and had been associated with gangsters and was undoubtedly a dangerous man.

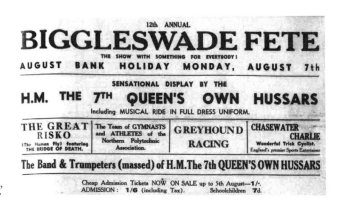

An advert from the *Biggleswade Chronicle* of Friday, 28 July 1933 announcing their annual fete. On the bill is the Great Risko otherwise known as 'The Human Fly.'

The Woolworth Building in New York City which was scaled by the Human Fly, George Polley. He climbed over 2,000 buildings in his career which spanned from 1910 to 1920.

By 1933, the 'Great Risko' was also being billed as the 'Human Fly.'

There were many other entertainers who took the name the Human Fly. These included Harry Gardiner (active 1905–1918) who climbed over 700 buildings in North America and Europe; 'Steeplejack' Charles Miller (active 1900-1910) who died after falling sixty feet from the fourth floor of the Hamburger building in Los Angeles as hundreds of spectators watched; George Polley (active 1910–1920) who climbed over 2,000 buildings including the Woolworth building in New York City; Henry Roland (active during the 1920s and 1930s) who climbed tall buildings all over America before being killed by a fall in 1937 and John Ciampa (active 1942–1952) who climbed tall buildings around his native Brooklyn and appeared in television broadcasts and movies.

All the acts, today are largely forgotten with the only ones gaining notoriety being the ones killed while performing.

Chapter Eight

The Great Raymond

The Great Raymond was born Maurice 'Morris' Saunders in Ohio in 1879. He was also known as Maurice Francois Raymond. When he was aged 9, his uncle, a touring magician, allowed him to travel with him one summer. His parents later forced him to return home to continue his schooling but let him join the circus the following summer and he found himself performing with the Stirk and Zeno Troupe of Aerialists in the Adam Forepaugh Circus. He then spent the following summer travelling with a different circus. By the age of 13, he toured as a boy conjurer on the Chautauqua and then the Kohl and Castle circuits. His grandfather took him to Europe and he later learnt magic from the country's fabled fakirs in India. Whilst there, he met Herrmann the Great and was much impressed by him.

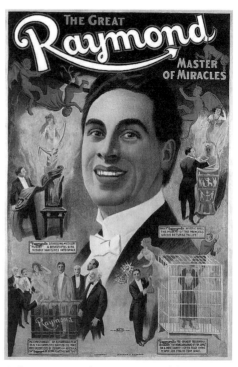

A theatre poster showing many of the Great Raymond's illusions. He was billed as the 'Master of Miracles'.

By 1904, The Great Raymond was touring the west coast of America and received good reviews. This led to him being offered a tour of the Orient in 1905. He toured England and Paris and set up a workshop in Europe. He also toured Australia and Asia. He was accompanied by a company of 30. While in Genoa, his wife left him and they later divorced. In February 1910, he was topping the bill of the Moss-Stoll tour in the UK. One of his most famous acts was 'Mytempsicosis' which was advertised as the fastest trunk escape in the world. He performed the illusion with his wife, Lipzka.

In 1913, he agreed a deal with John Cort, one of the largest theatre owners in America, to perform at $2 shows across the country. Raymond made about

An advert for the Great Raymond's forthcoming show at Burnley during December 1916.

$2,000 a week during the tour. Afterwards, he returned to Europe shortly before the outbreak of the First World War. For the next ten years, The Great Raymond toured Great Britain continually performing even during the war years.

The *Derby Daily Telegraph* of Thursday, 21 December 1916 carried the story of his appearance at the Grand Theatre. It read:

After an unavoidable delay of two days, this week's entertainment at the Grand Theatre opened to two splendid houses on Wednesday night. The premier attraction is 'The Great Raymond', an illusionist of the first water and one whose reputation is world-wide. It is six years since he visited Derby and in the interim, he has travelled the globe over, his feats of legerdemain gaining him admittance to the courts of Kings as well as the principal houses of entertainment in all lands. His magical powers were demonstrated on Wednesday night with telling effect and many new and original experiments are included in his programme. He introduces a 'throne of mystery' in which he substitutes various persons with extraordinary rapidity, while the original girl marches on to the stage from the audience. Another illusion which greatly mystifies the audience is that of an attendant vanishing in mid-air. He apparently hypnotises his subject, lays her flat on a table, and covers her with a sheet. Then the body floats in space, the table is removed and a large hoop is passed all round the figure, preparatory to the sheet being dragged away and the girl vanishing. These are but two of the innumerable feats, all of which excite amazement and mystification. The celebrated trunk trick, which nonplussed even Edison, is again introduced, and the speedy manner in which the manacled lady frees herself from the roped trunk, which when opened contains Raymond himself, is indeed something to marvel at, and impresses one with the fact that there is no illusion about the illusionist's ability. The other turns are also of interest and well back up the star artiste.

On Sunday, 1 February 1920, Harry Houdini's fellow members of the Magicians' Club presented Houdini with a scroll of welcome encased in a silver casket at a dinner held at the Savoy Hotel. The Great Raymond presided over the event which included performances from many well-known artists. Raymond had annoyed Houdini by ordering a Water Can for his act without Houdini's permission. Raymond apologised and admitted that Houdini was the founder of the escape. Tickets for the dinner were one guinea each.

A smiling portrait of the Great Raymond as featured in the *Evening Despatch* of Saturday, 6 January 1917.

Houdini was more interested in talking about the movies he was currently making than about his magic. He had filmed scenes in various cities around Britain which he planned to incorporate in a later movie. He stated that he planned to concentrate more on movies than stage work. Will Goldston recalled the event in his book *Sensational Tales of Mystery Men*:

I have already made some reference to the weaker side of Harry Houdini's nature, his childishness, his irritability, and his quick temper. While it is not my intention to stress the faults of one who for many years was a friend, I feel it is my duty to present to the public a true pen picture of the man as I knew him.

The weakness of Houdini's character was never better illustrated than at an annual dinner of the Magicians' Club, eight or nine years ago. We had decided that the gathering would provide a splendid opportunity of making him a presentation, for he had been our President since the inauguration of the club.

It so happened that the only available magician of any repute willing to occupy the chair and make the presentation was The Great Raymond. And Harry detested Raymond. 'I won't accept anything from that --,' he declared hotly. 'Why, he pinches my ideas,' and then he went on to tell me in a few well-chosen words just what he thought of Raymond's capabilities. I felt the position very keenly, but, to my relief, I managed to talk Harry over. I was a happy man when he finally agreed to allow Raymond to officiate.

We had several hundred cards printed for distribution amongst our members. But they didn't please Houdini.

'These are all wrong,' he said, when they arrived back from the printers.

'What's the matter with them?' I inquired wondering what my friend had at the back of his mind.

'You've got here "In the Chair – The Great Raymond." He's not great at all.'

'I shouldn't let that worry you. It's only a professional name.'

'Well it'll have to be altered. Call him just "M. F. Raymond." Even that's a damn sight too good for him. Don't let's argue about it, Will. Either you have these cards reprinted as I like them or I'll refuse to attend the dinner, and resign the presidency of the club in the bargain.'

There was no argument. The cards were reprinted.

The Great Raymond as shown in the *Aberdeen Press and Journal* of Friday, 20 May 1921.

Pearlitzka Gonser joined The Great Raymond's tour in 1924 and travelled the world with him. She played harp solos in the show and later assisted him in the stage illusions, 'Sawing a Woman in Half' and the 'Substitution Trunk' (Mytempsicosis). Litzka became his second wife when they married in 1927 on board the SS *American Legion*, seven miles off the coast of Montevideo, Uruguay.

He was still touring Britain in September 1924 when he appeared at the Theatre Royal in Lincoln. It was said that while touring, he had circled the globe seven times. He was shipwrecked twice, lost props for his show in the San Francisco earthquake, as well as losing his first show in a fire and had been involved in a railroad crash. He was also robbed and got caught up in two wars and several revolutions.

Raymond, along the way, fell out with Fu Manchu, the stage name of David Bamberg who claimed that he hadn't been fully paid by Raymond after a South African tour.

In the 1930s, he and his wife toured with Fanchon and Marco who provided shows for movie theatres. Their show lasted forty-five minutes and included eighteen dancing girls. The show began with The Great Raymond appearing in a flaming frame. Next, he

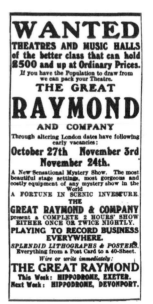

WANTED

THEATRES AND MUSIC HALLS of the better class that can hold **£500 and up at Ordinary Prices.** If you have the Population to draw from we can pack your Theatre.

THE GREAT

RAYMOND

AND COMPANY

Through altering London dates have following early vacancies:

October 27th   November 3rd November 24th.

A New Sensational Mystery Show. The most beautiful stage settings, most gorgeous and costly equipment of any mystery show in the World

A FORTUNE IN SCENIC INVESTURE.

THE

GREAT RAYMOND & COMPANY present a COMPLETE 2 HOURS' SHOW EITHER ONCE OR TWICE NIGHTLY. **PLAYING TO RECORD BUSINESS EVERYWHERE.**

SPLENDID LITHOGRAPHS & POSTERS. Everything from a Post Card to a 40-Sheet.

Wire or write immediately:

THE GREAT RAYMOND This Week: HIPPODROME, EXETER. Next Week: HIPPODROME, DEVONPORT.

An advert for the Great Raymond which appeared in the *Era* of Wednesday, 15 October 1924.

produced flowers from an empty bowl which he then threw into the audience. A trick with a box produced nine girls from an empty cabinet who then performed a parade, producing various animals from their drums. 'The Divorce Machine' illusion resulted in a girl vanishing from a chair suspended a few feet over the stage. The show closed with 'Mytempsicosis,' which he performed with Litza.

In 1932, he opened a talent agency in New York. He moved to Portland, Oregon where he became a technical advisor with the West Coast Film Company. He seemed unhappy with the movie business and said that it was destroying live performances. By 1945, he was in his mid-60s and semi-retired. He played a one-night show on Broadway which was the talk of the magic world. The show was well-received but was to be his last.

The Great Raymond died on 27 January 1948, aged 68, in New York.

After his death, Walter Gibson wrote in the *Conjurors' Magazine* about his friend saying,

The Great Raymond presented a 'Trip to Spookville' at the Palace Theatre in West Hartlepool in May 1925.

> With him has departed the Golden Age of Modern Magic, a period which knew such names as Herrmann, Kellar, De Kolta, Maskelyne, Devant, and others whose names will live forever in our art. For the Great Raymond was one of these; his was a name to conjure with.

However, Lloyd Jones wrote in *The Bat* of The Great Raymond:

> As a man though he made many enemies. His arrogant bearing, his outspoken prejudices, his lack of financial acumen coupled with many scrapes over money, his brutal treatment of his close associates and assistants, and his many idiosyncrasies will long be remembered. Truly, magic has lost a great name, a great figure, and a master magician but the world has not lost a beloved entertainment personality.

Chapter Nine

Will Goldston

Will Goldston was born in 1878 and was interested in performing magic from the age of 11. His birthplace is quite often given as Liverpool but it is thought that he was born near Warsaw, Poland.

His first job was as a dental technician but he made his stage debut as a magician aged 16. At the time, he used the name, Carl Devo. By the age of 21, he was topping the bill in many provincial theatres although his career didn't last long. He later became a magic dealer, an author, a publisher and an agent. He was great friends with all the popular illusionists of the day especially Houdini.

His brother, James Mayer Goldston, who died in 1905 of malarial fever in Calcutta, was also a magician who was known as 'Mokana'. He died aged 23 years while

A photo of a dapper-looking Will Goldston, complete with top hat and tails.

touring India with the Coronation Circus. Mokana invented the hollowed-out shoe heel which swivelled to reveal a secret space. Another brother, Reuben, was also a magician and toured the north-east of England.

Between 1905 and 1914, he was employed by Gamages department store in London in their magic section and sold magic tricks to the general public. At the same time, he edited the *Magician Annual* and in 1912 he wrote *Will Goldston's Exclusive Magical Secrets*. In 1911, he founded the Magicians' Club in London of which Houdini was a member. He sold magic tricks as William Goldston Ltd. and was based in Aladdin House, near Leicester Square, London.

He was an important part in many popular acts of the day and sold illusions to Chung Ling Soo as well as Houdini. Although associated with many illusionists, he fell out with most when he revealed the workings of their onstage tricks within the pages of his books. Houdini and Chung Ling Soo fell out over a Goldston illusion

A young portrait photo of Will Goldston.

A portrait picture of Will Goldston, complete with facsimile signature.

An invitation to the League of Magicians inaugural meeting during May 1911. Guests included Harry Houdini, Stanley Collins and Will Goldston.

An advert for the *Magician*, a monthly journal edited by Will Goldston. The advert appeared in the *Era* of Saturday, 19 January 1907.

called the 'Expanding Die'. Houdini said that he had the sole rights to the trick, however, Soo was performing the trick in Wales at the time. For ten years, Soo had been dismayed by Houdini's attacks on fellow performers and escapologists. Soo wrote to Houdini, 'I am not jealous of you, neither do I fear you!'

An advert from 1907 for Will Goldston's new book, *Latest Conjuring.*

The following year, Houdini performed the act for the first time in England.

The *Era* of Thursday, 1 February 1923 reported on a presentation given to Will Goldston by the Magician's Club:

For once, there were no illusions about the gathering of the Magicians' Club, at their headquarters, at the Dean Hotel, Oxford Street, on Wednesday of last week. All present were sincere in their appreciation of Will Goldston, the popular secretary, for they had met to present him with a testimonial.

Mr. Oswald Williams, who presided, declared that they had only just found Mr. Goldston out. He had had many business associations with him, and had found him to be, not only a fine businessman, but a very fine friend. 'Billy' was also a very benevolent man, the first to help a brother fallen by the way and the first to get others to help. When the club was first formed, he did an enormous amount of work, and incidentally gave of his money to get the club going. Why did he do all this? They had come to the conclusion that it was for his love for the conjurer and love for the club that had prompted him. In fact, without Will Goldston there would have been no Magicians' Club. Nobody else would have shouldered the work. To their shame they had only just found it out, to their credit they were going to recognise it. No fewer than 94 conjurers – an extraordinary list, all well-known, nobody missing – had subscribed to the testimonial. The difficulty was that they could not find out what Will wanted, although they had set spies to work. At length, one more brainy than the rest remembered that Will Goldston was moving and had expressed a wish to have a Wizard's Den, so they were going

An advert from 1916 for Will Goldston Ltd instructing people on how to apply stage make-up.

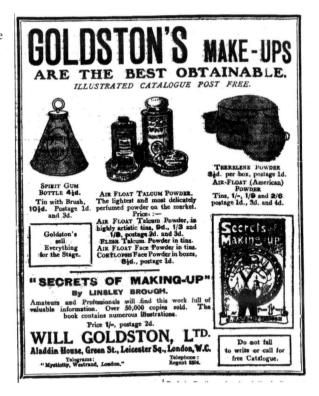

to furnish it for him. It was only a modest gift, but he was absolutely sure it would be valued by one of the finest fellows he had ever met.

Mr. Williams then handed a cheque to Mr. Goldston, who was greeted with musical honours and three cheers, with another for Mrs. Goldston, and the club mascot, Dolly.

Mr Goldston recalled how the idea of the club occurred to him in 1904 and described how he approached Carl Hertz, Lafayette, Houdini, and other famous illusionists with the proposal. The scheme matured, and in 1911, the club was opened with 40 members. They had a very nice club-room until war broke out, and then they could not make it pay. What they wanted to do was to get their own home again and he hoped each member would strive to introduce one, so that that end could be achieved. He thanked them all very much for their gift and hoped that when fitted they would all go along and see it.

Among those present, in addition to those mentioned, were Messrs. Nevil Maskelyn, G.W. Hunter, Ben Said, W. Melmore, W.G. Ling, Louis Gautier, Captain Van Der Kiste, Harry Heinhe, A.L. Fox and W.J. Minhinneck.

Goldston was known for cracking the 'Zancigs Code' which was used by Danish illusionists. He was also employed to expose fake mediums and spiritualists.

The story of his exposures was carried in the *Western Morning News* of Tuesday, 15 August 1933. It read:

Tricks adopted by bogus spiritualist mediums are exposed by Mr. Will Goldston, with the aid of the illusionist's professional knowledge, in 'Secrets of Famous Illusionists'.

Mr. Goldston's exposure is significant, because he declares himself a convinced adherent of spiritualism. 'I openly confess to a belief in things occult', he writes. 'At the same time, I agree that some fraud does creep into spiritualism, and there are, unfortunately, numerous bogus mediums preying on the credulity and inexperience of hundreds of men and women who are anxious for evidence from the spiritual world. In exposing some of the tricks practised by bogus mediums, my object is to help those mediums who are not what they profess to be.'

Anticipating objections from persons who have been deluded by a bogus medium, Mr. Goldston frankly states:

'If no precautions against trickery were taken, it is improbable that the medium was genuine; a true medium has no objection to such precautions, and most mediums in fact welcome them.'

Spiritualist trickery involves the possession of fairly complicated apparatus. Here is Mr. Goldston's description of a table on which spirits are supposed to tap:

'The top of the table is really a shallow box; the table can be thoroughly examined, and the medium can consent to its being placed in any part the room. In the foot of one of the legs of the table is a rubber bulb, painted to look exactly like the wood. Fitted to this bulb is a rubber tube ending in a little metal rod. To produce the mysterious taps, which he attributes to the presence of spirits, the medium has merely to sit at the table and press with his foot on the rubber bulb, causing the table rod to hit the underneath part of the table top.'

Another easy trick, states Mr. Goldston, is the answering of questions written on cards placed in sealed envelopes.

'Inside his waistcoat, near the top, the medium has two little pockets. Each holds a small sponge soaked in alcohol. Two pockets are necessary so that the medium may vary the movements of his hands at each reading. He merely has to get out a little sponge and pass it quickly over the envelope, which then becomes temporarily transparent. The medium can then read what is on the card inside the envelope. The alcohol quickly evaporates, and so at the end of the sitting envelopes can be examined if necessary.'

Materialization of a baby spirit Mr. Goldston describes as 'perhaps the foulest of all these wicked frauds'.

'The materialization is produced in total darkness or in very poor light. A small balloon, which the medium can easily inflate, serves as the baby's head. With a tiny telescopic rod the head can be made to 'float' at some distance from the medium. Draped round the head and falling from it, is some fine white Chinese silk, painted usually with luminous paint.'

He continued, 'The chief item in the stock-in-trade of a trickster of this sort is the supply of ordinary cheese cloth. The cheese cloth is soaked in water to take out the stiffening, and it is then so soft that it can be manipulated easily. As the material takes up little room in the pocket, a medium usually has two or three pieces of the stuff secreted on him, so that he may produce 'spirits' of different heights. One the most important pieces of apparatus in the tool-bag of a fraudulent medium is a pair of lazy-tongs. The ends of the tongs are fitted with a simple spring-grip, which can hold any light article, including a trumpet or even a ' ghost.' Another use for the lazy-tongs is to operate, at some distance from the medium, a tiny bellows, which creates draughts, attributed to the movement of spirits.

Many a poor victim has been deceived at a so-called spiritualistic seance by the spirit trumpet trick, which is really very good from the point of view of a magician. The medium has a number of flexible rods concealed in a special pocket down one leg of his trousers. To cause the trumpet to float about the room, all that the medium has to do is to take two or three rods from his concealed pocket, fit them into the trumpet, and wave it about. Luminous paint on the rim of the trumpet acts as a 'blinder' and makes the greater part of the trumpet invisible in the darkness.'

Mr. Goldston also describes how a man can apparently read a message in the dark, with the aid of a conical trumpet and a concealed electric light.

'Needless to say,' he concludes, 'fraudulent mediums are well aware that if they are not very careful their tricks may be discovered, and they are always trying to improve on their methods and to invent new ones.'

Goldston wrote seventeen mainstream books (although he compiled others), the last being *Tricks of the Master* in 1942. His book *Sensational Tales of Mystery Men*, published in 1929, gave an insight into the characters of many of the days' top illusionists.

Will Goldston died on 24 February 1948, aged 69, in Folkestone, Kent. He is buried at the Jewish cemetery in Dover.

Details of his will were published in the *Yorkshire Evening Post* of Saturday, 16 October 1948:

In the 51 books he wrote, Will Goldston, of Folkstone, founder of the Magicians' Club, described how nearly every famous trick was performed. But locked away were records of the secrets he did not disclose.

Among the bequests in his £3,027 will published today was one leaving 'the three locked books of exclusive magical secrets to Thomas Harris, of Boyer Street, Derby, for life, and then to the British Museum.'

Will Goldston was one of the most famous conjurers of his day. When 18, he performed before Queen Victoria. He taught conjuring to the Duke of Windsor when he was the Prince of Wales. Mr Harris told a reporter today: 'I have been supplied with two keys to Mr Goldston's books but of course, I can only allow accredited magicians to look at them.'

Chapter Ten

David Devant

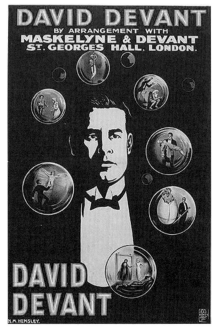

A theatre poster promoting the illusions of David Devant.

David Devant was born David Wighton in Holloway, London on 22 February 1868. He was a magician, a shadowgraphist and a film exhibitor. Devant performed regularly at the Egyptian Hall in Piccadilly, London as part of the well-known Maskelyne and Cooke company. In 1893, he was already top of the bill when he started to share the stage with John Nevil Maskelyne. By 1904, the pair were located at St George's Hall with their business and professional partnership commencing shortly afterwards. The union lasted for ten years.

Maskelyne and Devant's House of Magic became famous worldwide, and introduced the magicians of the day including Buatier De Kolta, Paul Valadon and Charles Bertram.

By 1905, he was in partnership with John Nevil Maskelyne and was eventually succeeded by Oswald Williams. During the same year, he invented the illusion 'Mascot Moth' which he thought to be his masterpiece. In front of the audience, a lady dressed as a moth would disappear the moment that Devant tried to capture her. Part of his show included the theatrograph, one of the first projectors, which was invented by Robert Paul.

The most astounding illusions were manufactured in Devant's storehouse of mysteries in Camden Town. This is where all the apparatus for the illusions was made. Anyone lucky enough to visit was not allowed to see much in case the game was given away.

He wrote several books about magic including *Our Magic*, *The Art in Magic*, *The Theory in Magic* as well as *The Practice of Magic* which was written with John Nevil Maskelyne in 1911. His home was in Hampstead, London. Today, a blue plaque marks the building.

He was a very popular entertainer in his day and appeared on the bill for the Royal Command Performance on three separate occasions. He was known for his magical inventions as well as humorous patter which accompanied his act. Queen Alexandra laughed out loud during his performance of 'A Boy, a Hat and Some Eggs' where Devant produced endless eggs which he gave to an assistant, chosen from the audience.

His name was used for the magic theatre owned by the Magic Circle in London. Ironically, Devant had been thrown out of the Magic Circle twice for revealing secrets of the trade within the pages of his books.

Devant was well-known for several illusions including 'The Magic Kettle' where he could produce, on demand, any alcoholic beverage suggested by the audience. Another favourite was 'The Moth and the Flame,' where he made a winged assistant spontaneously disappear.

The *Dundee Courier* of Tuesday, 4 June 1912 noted:

A school of conjuring in search of a 'professor' would choose, without hesitation, Mr David Devant. It is a long time since he was a pupil of the art. He graduated in the best company and seems now to have reached the limits of good-natured deception. Mr Devant renewed his acquaintance with Dundee in the King's Theatre last night. Splendid audiences assembled to give the king of magicians a welcome worthy of an artiste of his eminence, and everybody was mightily pleased with the wizard of the old Egyptian Hall. Mr Devant is not only a wonderful conjurer; he is a charming entertainer, who seldom opens his mouth without turning some polished subtlety. When assisted on the stage by children, Devant is delightfully natural. What a treat he would be at a children's party! Opening his entertainment last night, Mr Devant performed one of his oldest but still one of his best tricks. He calls it 'The Gollywog Ball'. Given an inclined plank and a big round ball, natural laws inevitably make that ball roll to the foot of the plank. Mr Devant in this trick defies gravitation. He makes the ball move at his will – up, down, slowly and quickly. Next, he performs a host of smart tit-bits of the conjuring business, every trick being accomplished in the most finished style. The big lines in Mr Devant's bill are 'The Artist's Dream', 'The Chocolate Soldier', and 'Peeps into the Past and Future'. These are 'the disappearing tricks par excellence'. Individuals vanish and reappear, and then vanish again – and the audience are still wondering how it is done. On Saturday afternoon, a matinee is to be given, consisting entirely of Mr Devant mysteries. There are other good numbers on the programme. Ernest Krake and his company of comedians create much fun in their comedy act, 'The Electric Tram Conductor', and Carl Lynn is a magnificent mimic of animals. Of him, it is literally true that he 'roars like a bull'. Enjoyable items are also provided by Sisters Royce and Syd, dainty vocalists and dancers; Lily Hayes, comedienne; Sisters Simms, vocalists and dancers; and Cummin and Seaham, acrobats'.

On July 1 1912, at King George V's command performance at the Palace Theatre in London, Devant was chosen to represent 'the world of wizardry'.

The *Yorkshire Evening Post* of Tuesday, 15 September 1914 mentioned his appearance at the Hippodrome:

David Devant, complete with moustache and fan.

Mr. David Devant who heads the bill at the Hippodrome this week, is the ideal conjurer. There is nothing of the loudly spectacular about his show, no blare of brass bands or waving of flags to distract the attention from the real thing, the trick he is performing. Instead, he does everything in quiet, whimsically humorous fashion which is most effective and bewilders his

A poster promoting David Devant's stage show.

A portrait shot showing David Devant, complete with upturned moustache.

audience absolutely by the sheer skill with which he does his work. The cutest would be unable even to guess how what are apparently the simplest of his tricks are done.

Fred Barnes, the well-known light comedy artist, also figures on the programme, and sings old songs and new with equal gusto and success. F. V. St. Clair, with a batch of topical, patriotic songs, gives a show which goes very well.

In 1915, Devant announced that he was retiring from the partnership Maskelyne and Devant Limited so that he could devote himself more to vaudeville work.

The *Exeter and Plymouth Gazette* of Tuesday, 27 November 1917 reported:

There were crowded and enthusiastic houses at Exeter Hippodrome last night, when David Devant, the world-famous entertainer and magician, opened a week's engagement, and already the bookings for the week are very heavy. Last night's performances were of extraordinarily clever character, and the magician was accorded a great reception at both houses, which, notwithstanding a turn of over an hour's duration, still clamoured for more. The mysteries last night were both artistic and bewildering. The first was the Golliwog ball, which was made to roll up and down a slanting board and to stop when required. A life-size German soldier was next placed on a pedestal, and surrounded with red, white and blue electric lights and flags of the same colours. At the signal from the magician, the flags were suddenly removed, and a very diminutive

An advert for David Devant's appearance at the Palace and Hippodrome in Burnley during April 1916.

A portrait photo of David Devant from the *Bedfordshire Times and Independent* of Friday, 9 November 1917.

A newspaper advert for *The David Devant Mysteries* which was published in 1923. The show featured 'indescribable surprises' and 'astonishing feats'.

An advert from 1920 for the all-British serial, *The Great London Mystery* starring David Devant and Lady Doris Stapleton.

figure was all that was left of the original Hun. A lesson in magic, in which a little boy took part, was remarkably clever, neat, and diverting. 'The Artist's Dream' was a remarkably clever performance, and the curtain was rung down amid prolonged applause on 'The Magic Mirror', which was, perhaps, the greatest mystery of all.

Devant was forced to retire in 1920 due to poor health although during 1923, the 'David Devant Mysteries' toured Great Britain, written by Devant himself and played to packed out houses. It was presented by Mr Woodhouse Pitman, assisted by Madame Stella and a full company.

The *Hull Daily Mail* of Tuesday, 27 November 1923 gave an account of the show:

After a long run of revues, there is a welcome return to variety at the Alexandra this week and the management are to be complimented on securing such a first-class programme. The David Devant Mysteries, of course, top the bill. The attraction is indeed world famous and justly it deserves to be. The disappearing tricks leave the audience astounded, almost aghast. Mr Woodhouse Pitman, who presents the attraction, makes a full-size teddy bear appear from a strong, empty box and later disappears from a pole in the middle of the stage. He then makes a real live toy soldier disappear, and in its place is left a tiny, little doll! He borrows a gentleman's watch, and that gentleman is on tenterhooks for a time. One very funny trick is the developing of real eggs especially when the eggs drop! The master mystery, however, is the artist's dream. Mr Pitman changes a picture to life in his sleep, the girl in the painting disappears again in place of the picture which returns, and then in the very centre of the front of the stage, another girl disappears in full gaze of an amazed audience! Here are mysteries enough for anyone to puzzle over.

On Wednesday, 28 March 1923, the *Gloucester Citizen* carried a report about a celebration for John Nevil Maskelyne's jubilee. It read:

Lord Knutsford, who has shown himself so expert in conjuring money out of people's pockets for the London Hospital, appeared at the St George's Hall in a different role on the night and surprised many by asserting that wizardry was his hobby as well as his profession. He made it quite clear, however, that he was not there to deceive anyone on that occasion and, to prove his words, handed to Mr Nevil Maskelyne a massive silver rose bowl and an illuminated address from the Magic Circle in honour of his – Mr Maskelyne's – jubilee as father of the magicians of England. Mr Maskelyne, replying, said that he only regretted that his own father, the founder of the family of magicians, was no longer alive to share the honour of the evening. Mr. J. N. Maskelyne, a Cheltenham watchmaker, came to London in 1873 after exposing, with his friend, Mr. Cook, those notorious Spiritualist mediums known as the Davenport Brothers. Maskelyne and Cook believed that, if they could manage to maintain themselves in London for three months, they would be able to tour the provinces with a London reputation and make a little money. But the entertainment they offered, much to their own surprise, caught the public fancy; they were soon obliged to look for a permanent London house and the association thus casually begun has lasted, in Mr. Maskelyne's case, for fifty years. Mr. David Devant joined the firm some seventeen years ago, and he was naturally a prominent figure at Monday night's celebrations. I do not think there is a more lovable personality in the magical world, nor one more generally beloved than David Devant. The feeling manifested at his opening speech, introducing Lord Knutsford to the audience, was intense and it broke all bounds at the end of Mr. Devant's new sketch. 'What did he do with the body?' which was presented on this occasion for the first time. It is a thrilling detective playlet showing how the sleuth tries to trap a murderer and how he fails owing to the latter's knowledge of wizardry. The inimitable Devant charm is over the whole thing in addition to which it is an extremely clever illusion.

By 1936, Devant was in the Putney Home for the Incurables when his book *Secrets of Magic* was published. He was again thrown out of the Magic Circle but allowed back in the following year.

His death was reported in the *Scotsman* of Tuesday, 14 October 1941:

David Devant, the conjuror and illusionist, died last night in a hospital in Putney, London, where he had been a helpless cripple for the past four years. He was 73.

Devant had been a houseboy at a private house, refreshment boy at Euston Station, telephone operator and gasfitter before he turned to conjuring. In 1920, he had to retire. Paralysis attacked him and made his dexterous hands useless. Some years later, he was asked to resign from the Magic Circle, who complained that he had infringed the rules by exposing some of his tricks in a book. He grieved over this. Subsequently, the Circle relented and begged him to return. He made it a condition that the twelve members should go to the hospital and entertain him. They did so and thereafter gave him a special birthday show there every year. Queen Mary sent him a birthday message last year.

Chapter Eleven

Carl Hertz

Carl Hertz was born Louis Morgenstein in San Francisco in 1859. He arrived in England before touring Europe with his magic show visiting Germany, Austria, Bavaria, Saxony, Hungary, France, Belgium and Holland. He later travelled to Australia and returned to England by way of China and India.

In the early years of cinematography, he introduced film shows as part of his act.

In 1884, he travelled to London and appeared at the Royal where he became a huge success. He relied, when he first arrived in England, on his reputation as the 'King of Cards'. His act included the disappearing canary trick and later 'The Vanishing Lady' illusion which he had purchased, he stated, from a Parisian mechanic. However, the illusion was soon being performed by every magician on the London stage and soon became 'old hat'. He made sure that his future illusions were all invented by himself and were patented so that no other act could steal his ideas. Hertz recalled:

The next thing I did was the Vanishing Lady, and finding that the public demanded sensational illusions I gave several, including 'Stroubaika,' my own invention which had a great run at the Alhambra. Ever since then I have been performing mostly in London. I have appeared before the Prince and Princess of Wales three times; I have a decoration from the Queen; and the Legion of Honour from the late President Carnot, for a performance given in Paris for a charitable institution. I have also given performances before the Emperor of Germany, before the late Crown Prince of Austria, and before the mad King Ludwick of Bavaria, he being the only occupant of the theatre.

As his fame rose, he also appeared at private functions, where he was very well paid. He was engaged by the Rothschilds and Vanderbilts to perform shows before them.

On 28 March 1896, Hertz sailed from England travelling on board the Royal Mail Steamer *Norman*. During the voyage, he exhibited Robert William Paul's Theatrograph to the passengers.

After visiting Australia, Lumiere Brothers employed him as a magician and he toured New Zealand, Ceylon, India, China, Japan, the Fiji Islands and Hawaii. He was assisted in his act by Emilie D'Alton, who was a vocalist, and who he later married.

A letter appeared in the *Lancashire Evening Post* of Friday, 16 December 1910 from a disgruntled audience member:

11, Fylde Street, Preston, December 13th.
To: The Manager, Hippodrome, Friargate.
Dear Sir, I witnessed the performance of Carl Hertz last night, and I am fully convinced that in the great Bird and Cage Trick, where he makes the bird and cage vanish in full view of the audience, that he must either kill or hurt the bird in doing the trick, and unless he can satisfy me by doing

MR.   CARL   HERTZ.
THE KING OF CARDS.

An early caricature of Carl Hertz published in 1887.

A portrait shot of Carl Hertz.

Carl Hertz performing his detached head illusion.

the trick with my bird, and returning it uninjured I will report it to the Society for the Prevention of Cruelty to Animals. Should he accept this challenge, he must agree not to touch my bird, and I must have permission to remain on the stage the whole of the time.

Yours faithfully, Matt Hopkins.

The newspaper went on to state: 'Carl Hertz has accepted the above challenge and agrees to give £50, if he fails, to any charitable institution of Preston that Mr Hopkins may suggest. The challenge will take place on Friday night (second house).'

The same letter, word for word, although signed by apparently different people, appeared in local newspapers up and down the country for at least the next ten years and was obviously written by Hertz himself. Almost identical complaints had been received since the late 1800s.

CARL HERTZ.

A portrait of a very young Carl Hertz published in the *Era* in 1900.

His famous 'canary trick' had made his name and was said to be his finest illusion and he had been performing it since the late 1800s. It involved him holding a canary in a collapsible cage. When he clapped his hands together, in a flash, the whole lot disappeared. In a moment the conjurer then produced the canary from behind a curtain, quite well and at ease. Many thought that the canary was killed during the act and concerns were raised about animal cruelty. The debate continued for the next eleven years. Hertz, however, had already performed the trick before the Society for the Prevention of Cruelty to Animals in the 1890s and had been issued with a certificate saying that the bird was unharmed. He recounted:

In 1884, I went to London, appearing at the Royal, where I met with wonderful success. The chief tricks I played then were with cards and the bird-cage trick, the latter of which I am doing now. This caused a stir, as the Society for the Prevention of Cruelty to Animals said that I killed a bird every time I did the trick. The proprietors of the music hall wanted me to stop doing the trick, as they feared they would lose their licence. After there had been a great deal of correspondence in the newspapers, which was really a splendid advertisement, I went to the Society's offices and offered to do the trick with one of their own birds and to return it to them afterwards, so that they could see if it were hurt or not. After a lot of controversy they agreed to this, and invited the representatives of the London press to their rooms. They put the bird into the cage for themselves. I did the trick twice, and they gave me a certificate to the effect that they had come to the conclusion that they were mistaken, and that no injury was done to the bird. After that the hall was crowded night after night; it was the biggest advertisement I had in London.

During the late 1800s and early 1900s, Hertz debunked mediums and spiritualism and appeared for the prosecution at the medium, Swami Laura Horos' trial in New York. In 1898, the court case was reported in the *Era*:

The most curious experience during his career was in New York, when he was appearing at one of the theatres. A remarkable case excited public attention. A woman, who proclaimed herself a spiritualist, obtained a hold on a very wealthy lawyer, who, except for his spiritualism craze, was a very intelligent man. She used her influence to get from him thousands of dollars. She would take a piece of blank paper and hold it against her forehead and then tell him to withdraw it. When he took it away there was writing on it urging him to give money for a spiritualistic temple. At another time, she had a clean writing-pad with blank leaves. She held two corners and he the other two. Then there was a sound of scratching, like writing, and on the pad being opened all the leaves were found to be written upon. By these and other means the woman had extorted many thousand dollars. At length his relatives stepped in, and the woman was prosecuted for fraud. 'I was called as a witness,' said Hertz, 'and did the very same things in the Court. When I was doing the pad trick with the lawyer himself, the woman shouted to him to tear a corner off one of the leaves. I asked him if he had done that when she held the pad. He said he had not. However, I agreed to his doing it, and he was greatly astonished to find the leaves written on. The scratching was done by splitting the nails, and the rest was merely a trick of substituting one pad for another. The woman was sentenced to two years imprisonment.

Hertz wrote regularly to Houdini about matters concerning spiritualism. The *Era* of Saturday, 27 January 1900 reported:

Mr Carl Hertz has abandoned the disappearing lady trick for a form of illusion which was popular in the old days of the Polytechnic and Egyptian Hall.

Carl Hertz at the Theatre Royal in Halifax in 1906 displaying his new illusion, 'The Bridal Chamber.'

Emilie D'Alton, a vocalist, was married to Carl Hertz and assisted him on stage.

A newspaper advert from 1904 promoting Carl Hertz's latest illusion, 'The Demon Kettle.'

It was then known as 'Mahomet's Coffin,' which was suspended in mid air without any visible means of support. The conjuror in this instance has elaborated the original idea very cleverly. Mdlle. D'Alton, as the recumbent figure, rests upon a trestle which is illuminated by powerful electric lights. A deep shadow is thrown upon the foreground of the stage,

An advert for Carl Hertz's show at the Palace and Hippodrome in Burnley during November 1915.

from which the trestle slowly rises by the aid of some mysterious agency. The conjuror last night passed a large steel hoop along the whole length of the figure to show that no supporting wires were concealed underneath the trestle. Mr Hertz contrives to make his entertainment additionally interesting by the introduction of some amusing conjuring tricks. Not a little fun was caused by the clever way in which the conjuror induced two somewhat reluctant members of the audience to mount the platform, in order to assist him with his tricks. Miss

Emilie D'Alton, as pictured in the *Dundee, Perth, Forfar and Fife's Popular Journal* of Saturday, 21 February 1914.

A newspaper portrait of Carl Hertz from December 1915.

D'Alton also personated the 'Mystic Chameleon' by standing at the back of the stage whilst coloured pictures of various national costumes were thrown upon her in rapid succession by means of an optical lamp.

During the First World War, Hertz toured Great Britain and Ireland extensively appearing in most towns and cities. The *Western Daily Press* of Tuesday, 4 January 1916 reported the return of the magician to the West Country:

A challenge to Carl Hertz from June 1914. A similar challenge, word-for-word, was published in every newspaper of every place that he visited.

Theatre Royal, Guildford
(Manager .... J. BAKER).

Sensational CHALLENGE to Carl Hertz.

J. BAKER, Esq.,
Theatre Royal,
Guildford.

27, George Road,
Guildford,
June 23rd, 1914.

DEAR SIR,

I witnessed the performance of CARL HERTZ last night and I am fully convinced that in the Bird and Cage Trick, where he makes the Bird and Cage vanish in full view of the audience, he must either kill or hurt the Bird in doing the trick, and unless he can satisfy me by doing the trick with my own bird and returning it to me uninjured, I will report it to the Society for the Prevention of Cruelty to Animals.

Yours faithfully,
E. PURDUE, Builder.

CARL HERTZ
has
accepted the Challenge—
and agrees to give

£50

to any Charitable Institution of Guildford that
Mr. Purdue may suggest
if he fails.

The Challenge will be met on FRIDAY NIGHT, June 26.
USUAL PRICES.

Carl Hertz, the mystery man, renewed his acquaintance with the Bristol Empire last evening, after an absence of 15 years, and his extraordinary exhibition of what may truly be described as wizardry will set deeply thinking those who help to crowd the popular Old Market Street music hall this week. In the course of a brief chat which the writer had with the well-known illusionist yesterday, reference was made to the somewhat Germanic sounding of the name, and to all who may have qualms on the subject, it may be explained that Hertz has lived in England and the United States all his life, and there can be no doubts as to which way his sympathies lie in the present war. Carl Hertz is, and has been, appearing weekly before wounded British soldiers from the time when the first of them arrived from the front. Postcards are sold by him every week for the purchase of tobacco and cigarettes for wounded Tommies at each of the local hospitals in the towns he visits. Mrs Hertz, moreover, has interested herself keenly, providing caps and scarves for the soldiers, and she supplies the wool to all who care to knit these useful and welcome articles of attire. That their joint efforts in these directions are appreciated is proved by the innumerable letters received from lads at the front. Carl Hertz is a singular personality – singular when his private and off-the-stage manner is contrasted with the opulent brilliance and unerring assurance of his performances. He is unassumingly entertaining in conversation and lacks all the pomposity which one might expect to experience at the hands of a mystery maker. He has had many adventures in foreign climes, as might be anticipated for a man who has travelled the world's circumference no fewer than four times. It must not be supposed that Hertz's capabilities as an illusionist are confined to the huge stage acts, such as the features of the present exhibition at the Empire comprise. He is nothing if not versatile, and his elaboration of mystery upon a large scale is equally matched by his deftness and artistic mastery of the minute details of expert palming. It is not surprising, therefore, that, such a man should be a terror to the nimble fingered gentry who, with plausible tongues and engaging graces, invoke the attention of the unwary globe trotter, and seek to fleece him during an apparently innocent game of cards. And this reminds the writer of an incident related by Hertz which occurred upon a well-known liner during a trip across the Atlantic. Hertz was invited to take a hand, and having his suspicions did so. His ideas to the characters of his companions were soon verified, and at the end of the voyage, a notorious gang of sharpers was exposed and taken particularly good care of.

A curious experience befell the magician in New York on one occasion. He missed his way from the theatre he was appearing at to his hotel, and did not arrive until very late. In the meantime, his friends became alarmed, and a typical American newspaper published the story of Hertz's death as the result of an accident. Hertz rang the editor up on seeing the obituary notice, and complained bitterly that such an item of false news would do him harm.

'Waal,' drawled the editor at the other end of the wire, 'I guess the only thing I can do is to give you a puff in the birth announcements tomorrow!'

On several occasions, Hertz has appeared before Royalty, and his valued souvenirs of such favours include presents handed to him from the late King Edward, the Dowager Queen of Spain, the Tsar of Russia and the Emperor of Japan. He, also, on one occasion received a valuable set of ivory from the hands of a certain cannibal king. His present performance is a succession of enigmatic acts. The War Map illusion is a speciality, the result of not a little concentrated thought and application of well-tried principles. Then, there are the Shell Nymph and the Rabbit and the Watch. Hertz does nothing which is not his own entirely, and he may, without question, be regarded as the most mysterious of mystery makers.

A newspaper portrait of Emilie D'Alton from the *Burnley News* of Saturday, 30 October 1915.

A newspaper portrait of a dapper Carl Hertz from October 1915.

On 2 August, 1921, he was summoned to the House of Commons to prove that his illusion, 'Vanishing Bird Cage' did not harm the birds involved in the act. He performed the trick in front of them and then produced the unharmed bird. He had successfully managed to continue the story of false cruelty to the bird for over 30 years. This brought him great publicity.

Another famous trick was his Indian rope illusion, for the execution of which Lord Lonsdale offered £1,000 in India without success. This trick took Hertz ten years to perfect. A coiled rope rose into the air, a small boy climbed up it, and then vanished as the rope fell to the ground. Vanishing ladies were also made popular

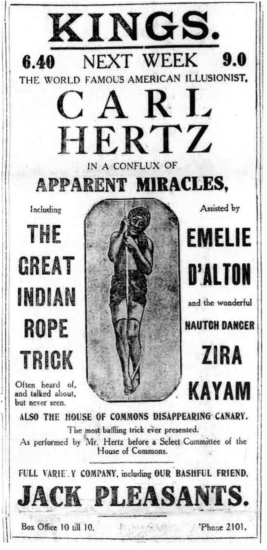

Carl Hertz in later life.

An advert for Carl Hertz's show at the King's Theatre in Portsmouth in May 1922.

A publicity photo of Carl Hertz.

on the music-hall stage by Hertz. Two assistants would take an empty case, show it inside and out and then a woman would step out of it, and afterwards disappear. His 'Merry Widow' illusion produced a woman out of a tent from nowhere onto a pedestal.

Hertz told a story that one night he was performing a favourite trick, squeezing a marked half-crown out of an orange, and then producing the coin from the pocket of a person in the audience. To a small boy on the far seat he called out:

'I think you'll find that I have passed the coin into your left hand trouser pocket.'

After fumbling nervously, the lad brought out a shilling, two sixpences and four pennies.

'That's not the half-crown,' said Hertz, uneasily.

'No,' said the boy. 'I was so thirsty, I took your half-crown to the bar as I came in, and had, a bottle of ginger beer.'

Hertz told newspapers an almost identical story but instead of a half-crown being mislaid, the tale included two white mice which had disappeared due the boy's cat having eaten them. Other illusions included 'Aerolithe' which showed a girl dancing on air; 'Vanity Fair' and 'Iris'. Another illusion, 'Phoenix' showed his wife entering a furnace and emerging unscathed. He was accused of stealing the illusion from a German magician and the matter was taken to court.

For forty years, Hertz performed in music halls and theatres all over Great Britain drawing in huge audiences. Hertz's autobiography, *A Modern Mystery Merchant: The Trials, Tricks and Travels of Carl Hertz, the Famous American Illusionist* was published in 1924, the year of his death.

Newspapers of Friday, 21 March 1924 carried short reports of his death: 'Carl Hertz, the well-known "illusionist", died at Coventry yesterday. He was giving a performance at a local house of entertainment and became ill. He was removed to a nursing home, where he died.'

Later, it was revealed that he had been a shrewd investor and had left a total of £200,000. However, this was later revealed to be an exaggeration and he actually left just £1,744.

Chapter Twelve

Horace Goldin

A photo of a young Horace Goldin.

Horace Goldin was born on 17 December 1873 and made his name as a stage magician most famous for his 'Sawing a Woman in Half' illusion and his lightning fast presentation style. He was born Hyman Elias Goldstein in Vilnius and was of Polish descent. When he was young, he had an accident which left him with a speech impediment. He became interested in carrying out magic tricks after being taught by a gypsy performer. His family, who were shopkeepers, moved to Nashville, Tennessee when he was 16 years old. He became a successful salesman despite his strong accent and speech impediment.

He was apprenticed to a travelling showman, Adolph Veidt, who persuaded him to change his name to Horace Goldin. In 1894, he began performing, combining jokes and magic tricks. He was billed as 'The Humorous Conjurer'.

At the start, he received poor reviews from newspapers but he proceeded with a new act, employing assistants and adopting a rapid presentation style, inspired by the German magician, Imro Fox. He became known as 'The Whirlwind Illusionist' and found success in vaudeville, touring America.

In 1901, he travelled to London and performed at the Palace Theatre. His shows were extremely popular and he was invited to perform a private show for King Edward VII and his guests at Sandringham in 1902. He appeared in a short humorous film, entitled *Comic Conjuring* in 1905 which was made in the UK.

Goldin continued to tour up and down Great Britain for the next ten years, appearing at major theatres and music halls. At the outbreak of the First World War, he was still touring but left England the following year. By the end of 1915, he was touring the Far East. Newspapers reported that 'he had made good in

Bombay,' where he performed the 'Tiger God' trick which included a live tiger on the stage.

By August, 1916, Goldin had arrived in Australia and appeared in theatres to much acclaim. While on tour in 1918, the boat he was travelling on sank at Lahaina, Hawaii. It was not only carrying all his equipment but also all of his earnings which were lost in the disaster. He distrusted banks and carried all his money with him, reputedly in gold bars. Bankrupt, he returned back to England.

His bankruptcy was reported in the *Edinburgh Evening News* of Friday, 14 November 1924:

> Creditors of Horace Goldvein, better known as Horace Goldin, the illusionist, met yesterday at London Bankruptcy Court under the receiving order made against him on his own petition a fortnight ago. Debtor said he was a naturalised American of Russian birth. During 1910-1912, he was in England experimenting in his profession, and was persuaded into borrowing from moneylenders, who were 'always badgering him'. The war greatly affected his earnings. In 1915, he toured in the Far East, and in his absence his landlord distained on his effects and sold them. In 1918, he lost some £5000 worth of baggage while joining a liner for America. He had not lived extravagantly. His theatrical properties, which had cost him thousands, were placed in store, and about a year ago, they were sold for under £100. He was now performing under contracts arranged by a company.
>
> He attributed his failure to heavy interest on borrowed money, and to loss in experiments and on professional business owing to war. He estimated his liabilities at £9000 and his assets at £2, plus 36 dollars in an American bank.
>
> The case was left with the Official Receiver.

His career took off with his development of the 'Sawing a woman in half' illusion. He was credited with the act but it was an improvement on an illusion previously performed by a British magician, P T Selbit. However, Goldin patented the act and sued any competitors. Patenting the act meant that he had to reveal the trick's secrets and these were given away by a tobacco company some years later. Goldin tried to sue but the case was eventually dismissed by a federal court in 1938.

His show was mentioned in the *Exeter and Plymouth Gazette* of Tuesday, 17 March 1925:

> It is some time since an illusionist topped the bill at the Exeter Hippodrome. Therefore, the visit of a star turn of this nature is in itself interesting, but when, as in the case this week, Horace Goldin is the visitor, the engagement becomes one of great interest and importance. The name of Horace Goldin,

'the King of Magicians and the Magician of Kings', is known throughout the world, for not only is he the inventor of some of the most ingenious illusions of the day, but the lavish and attractive manner in which he stages his performance renders it unique in the world of magic.

Horace Goldin, whose illusions have mystified crowned heads, as well as music-hall audiences in all quarters of the globe, has brought his full company to Exeter under the direction of Mr H. Myers, I.M.C., and his engagement constitutes the 'event of the season' as far as the Hippodrome is concerned. Goldin is a born showman, he mystifies and entertains at one and the same time. The opening part of his performance includes some remarkable tricks with animals, birds and fish. Horace Goldin

A theatre poster advertising Horace Goldin's latest show promoting his 'Sawing a Lady in Half' illusion.

casts a fishing line over the heads of people in the front seats, and as he withdraws it, a goldfish is seen at the end of it, and a second later, the fish is disporting itself in a bowl of water. The illusionist 'catches' several fish in this extraordinary fashion. Very effective and clever are tricks in which large pieces of cloth tied together are separated by the illusionist passing his hand along them. There are several other minor tricks of a novel and interesting character. The principal illusions, however, are the Oriental rope trick, 'from film to life', and the 'Sawing through of a woman'. In the first mentioned, a man climbs a rope, in full view of the audience, is covered with a cloak, the cloak is withdrawn, and the man is – where? Gone! In the film illusion, Horace Goldin introduces a little clever protean work. Standing beside the screen, he participates in the plot of the film, and eventually, a lady 'steps out' of the film screen on to the stage. She is smoking a cigarette handed to her film photograph by Goldin. It is novel and clever. As regards the 'sawing through of a woman', Horace Goldin invented this illusion, and, although other entertainers have copied it, their manner of presenting it is far less

Horace Goldin on stage performing his levitation illusion. He is seen passing a hoop over his subject to show that there are no hidden wires.

EMPIRE

6-45 — TWICE NIGHTLY — 8-45
TO-NIGHT (WEDNESDAY) AND DURING THE WEEK.

SPECIAL VISIT AT GREAT EXPENSE OF THE WONDERFUL

HORACE GOLDIN,
ROYAL ILLUSIONIST, IN SILENCE AND THRILLS.   A SHOW IN HIMSELF.

PRESENTING THE GREATEST ORIGINAL AND LATEST MYSTERIES EVER ATTEMPTED

Sawing a Woman in Half—

Miss Peggy Beeney, of 102, Cecil Street, Manchester, has challenged Horace Goldin to let her take the place of the lady in the Box and be sawn in half. Mr. Goldin has accepted the challenge and the test will take place at the first house on Friday night.

SUPPORTED BY ALL STAR VARIETY COMPANY EDITH WILSON, X. L. DEXTER, BARRETT & S...
HORSBURGH BROS., GLYNN GRAFTON.

BERT MADDISON AND BETTY CRICHTON.

PRICES — STALLS 1/6 (Booked 2/3); CIRCLE 1/- (Booked 1/3); PIT 8d. (Early Doors 1/-); GALLERY 4d. 6d.

NEXT WEEK "JUST FOR FUN." FEATURING GEORGE WE...

An advert for Horace Goldin's show at the Empire in Burnley during May 1927.

convincing than is the inventor's. A lady is lowered into a box in a sling. Her feet protrude from one end of the box and her head from the other. Two members of the audience, selected by a method which precludes any chance of confederates being employed, go upon the stage. One holds the feet and the other her head. One of the lady's stockings is cut and turned back to prove definitely that a human leg is inside it. The illusionist saws through the middle of the box, parts it, and walks through it. All the time, the two members of the audience retain their hold of the lady's feet and head. The two portions of the box are again united, the sling comes down again, and the lady is hoisted aloft, free from any harm.

A photo of an older Horace Goldin, complete with cigar.

It is a bewildering illusion. Horace Goldin performs a host of other baffling tricks, and the audience goes home spellbound.

Goldin blamed the cost of lawsuits for eating up the proceeds of his inventions. However, he was paid well and was said to have made a million dollars for the

Keith theatre group. His own pay was about $2,000 a week. He toured the world with his various variations of the sawing illusion. Altogether, he performed in front of King Edward VII on four occasions, which earned him the billing, 'The Royal Illusionist'. He also appeared before US presidents Harding and Wilson.

The *Derbyshire Times* of Friday, 24 February 1939 reported on Goldin's latest show:

Horace Goldin, the illusionist, brings his road show to the Hippodrome next week. This remarkable magician will present his latest trick of catching between his teeth a bullet from a gun fired by a member of the audience. He will also disappear with the lights fully on. Mr Goldin, who recently returned from a world tour, has a delightful story to tell of an experience while on his way across the Atlantic from New York on one occasion. He was watching a game of poker in the smoking-room and saw two wealthy young men, one an American and the other an Englishman, being 'fleeced' by card sharpers. They lost £650 between them. When they backed out, Mr Goldin stepped in. He began as an innocent stranger, stipulating low stakes. His first act was to 'palm' the Ace of Hearts while shuffling. As the game progressed and he was allowed to win, he added the King, Queen and Knave of Hearts to the Ace. Then he saw that the sharpers were up to their old tricks again, dealing good hands to one another. Mr Goldin went on winning steadily. Finally, he was dealt with the three, four, five and six of hearts. The fifth card was the knave of diamonds – and the dealer had seen the cards. Mr Goldin's hand needed a two or a seven to make it almost unbeatable. The betting went on until Mr Goldin had raised the stakes to 1,000 dollars and there was only one of the 'sharpers' left in. Finally, the 'sharper' put down 2,000 dollars and said 'I'll see you', at the same time showing his hand – three fours and two sixes. Mr Goldin put down his cards – but by the time his cards were on the table, the knave of diamonds had miraculously changed into the joker, which counted as everything. Mr Goldin won! Then the magician called the two young men to him and told them to help themselves from his winnings and take out the cash they had lost. He pushed the rest of the money back to the cardsharpers, made a pass with his hands and produced two kings, a queen and a knave. The 'sharpers' could make no protest!

On 22 August, 1939, Goldin died at his home soon after performing a show at the Wood Green Empire Theatre in London. On the night, he successfully performed the bullet catch trick which had killed his fellow performer, Chung Ling Soo, on stage twenty-one years earlier.

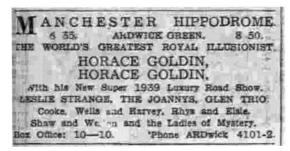

An advert for Horace Goldin's show at the Hippodrome in Manchester during May 1939.

Horace Goldin's death was reported in the *Dundee Evening Telegraph* of Tuesday, 22 August, 1939. The article read:

A portrait of a serious-looking Horace Goldin pictured in 1939.

Horace Goldin, the illusionist, died suddenly in London early today shortly after returning from performing at a North London music hall. He was about 65.

Goldin, described as 'the world's greatest magician', was famous for his feat of 'cutting' a woman in two with a circular saw and among his many other illusions, he claimed to have mastered the Indian rope trick, the secret of which he declared he obtained from one of the disciples of a yogi in Rangoon.

Less than two years ago, Mr Goldin published his autobiography – *It's Fun to be Fooled* – in which he told how he performed before King Edward VII and Queen Alexandra, other members of the Royal family and the ex-Kaiser.

'The egg-in-the-bag trick was the high spot of the evening,' he wrote. 'It seemed to me that His Majesty knew that it required great skill to deceive the audience at such close range. It was the King himself who held my hands for the trick. I asked the King to feel inside the bag and while his hand was still inside, I produced the egg.'

Mr Goldin also told how he had the assistance of the Duke of Connaught and Queen Alexandra in performing a card trick.

Chapter Thirteen

Harry Kellar

Harry Kellar was born Heinrich Keller in Erie, Pennsylvania in 1849. His parents were German immigrants. From the late 1800s, he toured as a magician and performed elaborate stage shows, appearing all over the world.

As a youth, while experimenting with various chemical concoctions, he blew a hole in the floor of his employer's drugstore. Rather than face the wrath of his parents and employer, he boarded a train and lived the life of a vagabond. On the road, he encountered the Fakir of Ava who inspired him to take up conjuring.

His act included several well-known illusions. One of them, 'The Vanishing Birdcage' was invented by Buatier De Kolta. Kellar purchased the idea in the 1870s for $750, an incredible amount of money at the time.

The 'Vanishing Lamp' was also a very popular illusion performed by Kellar in which he covered a lit lamp while it was standing on a glass-topped table. The light of the lamp could be seen through its covering cloth. Kellar would tell the audience that the lamp belonged to a Brahmin High Priest from India and had to be returned to him at a certain time. A bell would chime out and at that time, Kellar would load a pistol which he would fire at the lamp. In front of the audience, the lamp would then melt away and the cloth would fall to the ground.

Kellar also performed the levitation illusion 'Princess Karnack'. After Kellar's death, the illusion was bought by Harry Blackstone Snr and was performed successfully for many years after.

His wife, Eva, assisted in many of his illusions.

A theatre poster promoting Harry Kellar's latest illusion, 'Self Decapitation'.

A poster promoting Harry Kellar's illusion, 'The Witch, the Sailor and the Enchanted Monkey.'

Will Goldston wrote about Kellar in his book *Sensational Tales of Mystery Men*:

With the possible exception of Houdini, it is doubtful if America ever produced a finer or more clever showman than Harry Kellar. He was a man who knew his work from A to Z, and his ability, coupled with a most delightful personality, made him an exceedingly popular figure on the American stage. He never performed in England, but his name was well known here, and many of his finest and most bewildering illusions were inspired by private visits to this country.

Kellar was an excellent business man, and conceived the idea of running his own road show. His confidence in this scheme was amply justified, and he amassed a considerable fortune by touring the larger towns of the United States. I have never yet met the man who saw him play to a poor house.

But, strange as it may seem, Kellar departed from all the accepted rules of honesty and fair play when it came to choosing tricks for his programme. If he saw an illusion which appealed to him, he would get it, if not by fair means, then by foul. I will do him justice by saying that he always first attempted to strike an honest bargain over such deals. If his preliminary

A portrait shot of a serious-looking Harry Kellar.

Harry Kellar, in later years, with his pet dog.

overture failed, he would find out, either by bribery or close observation, how the trick was performed. Then, when a suitable period had elapsed, he would incorporate it into his own programme.

I can remember such an occasion about thirty years ago, when Hercat was performing the famous 'Blue Room Mystery' in London with considerable success. Kellar, who was visiting this country at the time, saw Hercat's show, and decided the trick would do splendidly for presentation in the States. He approached Hercat with a view to buying the mystery, but the latter – a keen business man also – refused to listen to his proposals. But that didn't worry Harry in the least. Shortly afterwards Kellar staged 'The

An older Harry Kellar pictured with Houdini.

Blue Room Mystery' in America with all the polish and effect of his rival's London show!

On 16 May, 1908, he performed his last show at Ford's Theatre in Baltimore before retiring, naming his successor as Howard Thurston.

On 11 November, 1917, Harry Houdini persuaded Kellar to return to the stage for one more performance. The show benefited the families of the men who died on board the ill-fated troop transport vessel, *Antilles*, which had been sunk by a German U-boat. At the end of the performance, Kellar was carried off stage in triumph while 6,000 spectators sang 'Auld Lang Syne'.

Little was mentioned of Harry Kellar's death in the British press. The *Yorkshire Evening Post* of Saturday, 11 March 1922 carried a small paragraph which read: 'From Los Angeles, the death is announced, in his 73rd year, of Mr. Harry Kellar, the famous public entertainer, who had been performing in leading American cities for the past 37 years.'

Chapter Fourteen

John Clempert

John Clempert was born in Russia in 1878 and was a professional wrestler before he decided to try his hand at being an escape artist. He was billed as 'The Man They Cannot Hang' and performed an illusion where he dropped fifteen feet with a rope around his neck.

His career began at Ferroni's Circus where he appeared as a wrestler and performed feats of strength with his teeth.

In 1903, while performing the hanging trick, he had an accident which ended his 'The Man They Cannot Hang' career. The stunt was dangerous and it seemed inevitable that his act would go wrong as it did one night in Rochester when he injured his spine. While recovering in bed, he decided that he would perform an act similar to Houdini's which included escaping from prison cells, handcuffs and chains. Taking his cue from Houdini, he developed an escape act and billed himself as 'The Handcuff and Siberian Gaol Breaker'.

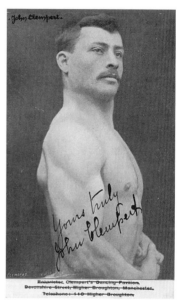

A portrait of a young John Clempert showing off his physique.

He joined Warren's American Circus in 1904 and toured India and the Far East as well as making a few appearances in England. His show imitated that of Houdini's and included an exposé of his Milk Can Escape. Variety acts were protected by copyright in England and Houdini sued Clempert who later apologised. Many think that Clempert disappeared from the scene after his feud with Houdini but he continued his act with similar stunts and appeared all over the UK. The Milk Can Escape became 'Escape from a Submarine', for instance.

From 1907 until 1914, Clempert regularly appeared on stages throughout Great Britain. He toured with his wife, Nellie. Before they met, Nellie had appeared on stage as one half of the Carson Sisters, a song and dance act. They had four children including David, Maurice, Zelda (later an actress and playwright, Zelda Davees) and Aron.

The *Manchester Courier and Lancashire General Advertiser* of Wednesday, 14 April 1909 reported: 'John Clempert, an athlete who is this week appearing at a London music hall and claims to rival Houdini, "the Handcuff King", was prevented by the police yesterday from diving from Tower Bridge for a wager.'

The *Sheffield Independent* of Thursday, 15 April 1909 reported on Clempert's appearance in court:

John Clempert's 'Escape from a Submarine' stunt.

John Clempert, the Russian music hall artiste, who, it had been announced, would dive from Tower Bridge in manacles on Tuesday, but who was arrested by the police before he could do so, was brought before Alderman Howse, at the Mansion House Police Court, yesterday, on a charge of disorderly conduct. Mr A A Strong defended.

Sub-Divisional Inspector Hopkins, of the Tower Bridge police station, said that at ten minutes past one on Tuesday afternoon, the defendant, who was in swimming costume, with handcuffs and chains on him, drove in a cab on to the bridge, and witness suspecting what was about to happen, ran after the cab. The pavement was thronged with people and several men shouted to the defendant to get out and do it from the other side.

Witness called to the cabman to stop and he did so. Defendant asked: 'What right have you to stop me?' and witness replied: 'I believe you are going to jump from the bridge and you will not be allowed to.' Defendant became very excited and several times shouted: 'Are you going to pinch me?' A large crowd gathered round and eventually the defendant got out of the cab.

He was asked to go away but refused to do so and was arrested for being disorderly by causing a crowd to assemble.

Mr Strong said that the defendant was a Russian and was accustomed to performing similar feats in his own country. He had made a wager to dive from the bridge.

The Alderman said he could not see what possible defence there was to a charge of disorderly conduct. 'You don't mean to suggest,' he asked, 'that a man can be permitted to go to Tower Bridge and amuse himself by jumping in the river with handcuffs?'

Mr Strong: 'He did nothing of the sort. I do not think, at the moment he was stopped, he had any intention of diving from the bridge. He is a foreigner and does not understand what a terrible crime it is in this country to cause a crowd to assemble.'

The defendant was bound over in £50 to keep the peace for six months.

In 1909, he wrote a book entitled *Thrilling episodes of John Clempert: the shining star of the realms of mystery*.

The *Motherwell Times* of Friday, 29 August 1913 carried a report of one of his shows at the Hamilton Hippodrome:

There are audiences of very gratifying numbers at the Hippodrome this week, the usual high-class variety and picture programmes having been resumed for another season. The large and enthusiastic audience we saw there the other night augurs well for the success of this establishment for the present and future. A good many Motherwell people have long been in the habit of visiting the Hamilton Hippodrome, and it looks as if it still retains their favour, for we recognised a good percentage of Motherwellites amongst those present. Mr Bostock heads his bill with a genuine sensational novelty – Mr John Clempert's amazing act entitled 'Saved from a Living Death in Siberia'. Mr Clempert demonstrates, in full view of the audience, how he escaped from a Russian torture jacket. Amongst his other marvellous feats is his 'Escape from a Submarine', a thing apparently beyond explanation. There is a welcome appearance of Mr George Rae, the eccentric Scottish comedian, who quite makes the audience roar with his 'Ach Away' and other entertaining songs. Miss Lily Hill, aptly described as the Lancashire Nightingale, has an excellent reception, have also Keen and Waller, a very original pair of eccentrics. King and Carson are a couple of new-style comedians whose efforts meet with high appreciation. Direct from the West End Playhouse, Glasgow, we have the wonderful 'Five Sollies', in a dazzling and versatile vaudeville novelty. Last, but not least, Cowboy Williams, a real son of the prairie, gives a decidedly clever entertainment in the role of a cowboy juggler. Amongst the pictures shown on the Hippodrome bioscope is a particularly fine drama entitled, 'A Victim of Heredity'.

In April 1914, Clempert was appearing at the Palace in Arbroath where he was billed as 'The Napoleon of Mystery'.

With the outbreak of the First World War, Clempert disappeared from the public eye but made a re-appearance in 1927 (a year after Houdini's death) and performed magic and escapology. During the war, Clempert joined the army, rising to the rank of Sergeant in the Royal Fusiliers. It was reported in newspapers that he was also the inventor of the steel helmet.

After the war, he and Nellie had a son, Aron, who was born on 12 November 1918. Aron would later change his name to Glenn Melvyn and became a well-known actor, scriptwriter, producer and director. He worked in film, television, theatre and radio, and was well-known for writing comedies and farce during the 1950s.

What Clempert got up to during the period from the end of the war until 1927 is unknown.

The Stage of Thursday, 24 February 1927 announced his return: 'After ten years' absence from the profession, John Clempert has returned with a new act. His escapes from seemingly impossible positions have caused lively interest at the Pavilions, Southport and he reports success for his new items.'

The *Hull Daily Mail* – Tuesday, 14 February 1928 reported:

Admirable entertainment is provided at the Alexandra Palace this week by a high grade variety programme headed by John Clempert described as the 'Napoleon of Mystery', who presents many novel and thrilling feats. Doubly handcuffed, he escaped from a locked mail bag from under the eyes of a vigilant committee and

THE

PALACE.

Sole Proprietor—Mr ARTHUR DEAN.

7—TWICE NIGHTLY—9

Monday, April 20th, and during the Week.

The Great Eastern Railway Co.
have at last found and delivered
John Clempert's Goods.

To avoid disappointment, arrangements have bee
made for

JOHN   CLEMPERT

To produce his Sensational Mystifying Act at
Each Performance Next Week.

SAVED FROM A LIVING DEATH
IN SIBERIA.

Sensational and Mystifying Production by

CLEMPERT,

THE NAPOLEON OF MYSTERY,

Direct from the Principal Halls, in his Repertoire o
Sensational and Unique Death Defying Escapes, wil
repeat exactly as it occurred, his Marvellous Escape fron
a Russian Torture Jacket, in Full View of the Audience
The Jacket is identical with that used to torture prison
ers by the Russian Government. The Great India
Needle Mystery. Would you believe me or not Puzzle
Have you ever been Locked Up? Catch me am I stil
Locked. Don't give it away. The Leather Bag Sensa
tiod. £100 if you can find false seams. Also his Latest
Invention, THE ESCAPE FROM A SUBMARINE
filled to the brim with hot water, and locked with 3 Pad
locks, demonstrating to the Public in full view, the
Escape from Hardcuffs, and Changing Costume unde
water. A Committee from the audience will be specially
invited. Bring your own Padlocks. THE FEARLESS
CLEMPERT STANDS UNRIVALLED. Owing to his
Large Repertoire he will vary his Performance Nightly.

Entire Change of Pictures

MONDAYS.   THURSDAYS.   SATURDAYS

Entire Change of Pictures Each House on
SATURDAYS.

An advert promoting John Clempert's show at the Palace in Arbroath during April 1914.

later from a strait-jacket, while swinging in mid-air. This is not all, for he performs startling exploits equally spell-binding.

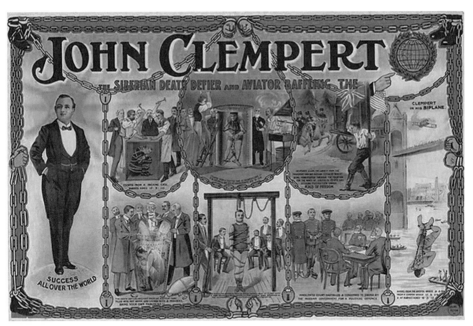

A theatre poster promoting John Clempert, 'The Siberian Death Defier and Aviator.'

In many ways, Clempert's act was just as impressive as Harry Houdini's. However, today, Clempert is far less well-known.

The *Lincolnshire Chronicle* of Saturday, 15 March 1930 advertised Clempert's show as an 'enormous attraction'. He played for six nights in the town to packed audiences. After this date, nothing is mentioned of him in the local press. By 1930, he would have been 52 and perhaps too old to still be performing escapology acts.

He died ten years later in 1940. His death went mainly unreported in British newspapers. Things had moved on. By 1940, escapology acts were a thing of a bygone age and the cinema had long since replaced the music hall and the new celebrities of the day were no longer variety acts but movie stars.

Chapter Fifteen

Dr Ormonde

Dr Ormonde was born Andrew Garrioch Ormond in about 1841 in Kirkwall, Scotland.

In 1878, he briefly worked as an assistant to Signor Blitz, whose father, also called Signor Blitz (1810-1877), was renowned for performing the Bullet Catch stunt. Blitz was an accomplished magician who was born in Deal, Kent. His act included magic, illusion, ventriloquism and juggling. He claimed to be Moravian because he thought it would get him more work.

The Ormonde family toured in mainly England, Scotland and Ireland in the late 1800s and incorporated some of Blitz's ideas into their act. Dr Ormonde was billed as the 'king hypnotist in the world'. His family known as the 'La Belle Sunflower Company', consisted of Mdlle Stella Ormonde (clairvoyant and Dr Ormonde's wife), Miss Lottie Ormonde (violinist and daughter), Percy Ormonde (musician and son) and Mr Fred Ormonde (lightning cartoonist and son). Mdlle Stella Ormonde also performed bewildering Japanese, Indian and Chinese illusions. The family claimed to have toured America, Australia and India but the only newspaper reports of their appearances show them as travelling in just England, Scotland and Northern Ireland. Like many illusionists and magicians of the time, some of their accomplishments were probably greatly exaggerated.

The *Cork Constitution* of Wednesday, 28 December 1887 reported:

On last evening, a small and very noisy audience assembled to witness a performance by the Ormonde Family in the Assembly Rooms. The entertainment differs in a great many respects from that what is usually associated with latter conjurers. It has several unique attractions of its own and there is around the whole an air of variety and mystery that is sure to please if it does not wholly satisfy. Dr Ormonde performs a series of excellent high-class illusions; his method is pleasant and artistic. Mr Fred Ormonde gives a very clear ventriloquial entertainment and creates much amusement with his mechanical speaking figures. The same young gentleman afterwards fairly astonishes the audiences by the marvellous rapidity with which he executes cartoons of celebrities of the age. Miss Lottie Ormonde, a little girl of about eight, plays with exceeding brilliancy a number of selections on the violin. Her execution is marvellously facile. Miss Stella Ormonde gives some very striking illustrations of thought-reading. Blindfolded and cushioned in a sheet on the stage, she describes articles of jewellery etc selected at random from the audience, and which she could not possibly have seen. She subsequently gives sensational manifestations in a cabinet, or what is familiarly known as the 'dark séance'. In this instance, however, it is performed in the light. The Ormonde family will remain in Cork until next week, and no one who desires to spend a pleasant evening should miss seeing them.

From the 1880s onwards, they toured theatres in Scotland and the north of England. The show remained much the same for many years and included magic, illusion, clairvoyance, violin playing and cartooning.

The family appeared on stage in Hastings in 1896. Dr Ormonde produced flowers galore from plates and gave astounding revelations using a spirit hand which mystified the audience. Fred performed an act of ventriloquism while manipulating six mechanical figures and Lottie played a violin made by Kiaposse of St Petersburg in 1748 which was valued at £650. She was later accompanied by Percy on a Hungarian cimbalom. Later in the act, Lottie, while asleep, worked out numbers to the square and cube while Stella provided psychic answers to questions from the audience concerning lost property, relatives, husbands and lovers.

DR ORMONDE.

A newspaper portrait of Dr Ormonde published in 1895.

Some thought that the Ormondes were in league with the devil as reported in the *Ipswich Journal* of Saturday, 29 February 1896:

The Ipswich Lecture Hall was crowded, as it has very rarely been, and a throng of people were turned away, on Friday evening, when the Rev. T. I. Jarrott offered a criticism on Dr. Ormonde's entertainment. The lecturer said he heard that certain persons had come to make a disturbance, but he had too great a faith in the fairness of an Ipswich audience to credit that statement for a moment. (Cheers.) He explained that the reason he had not arranged this gathering before was that he had not any knowledge of Dr. Ormonde's

MDLLE. STELLA ORMONDE.

A drawing of Mdlle. Stella Ormonde from 1895.

proceedings until close upon the time that he was leaving the town. The reason he took the matter up was because of the extraordinary influence which Dr. Ormonde exerted. One person advanced the absurd theory that Dr. Ormonde was in league with the evil one. (Laughter.) After stating that he went to one of Dr. Ormonde's lectures, on Wednesday week, to learn for himself what was being done, Mr. Jarrott said the first thing that struck him was the time that elapsed between the questions and answers. He wrote to Dr. Ormonde before the Thursday entertainment to say he was coming. When he got inside two men were waiting with a vacant chair for him.

Asserting that this was not a new entertainment, Mr. Jarrott quoted Truth regarding an entertainment by a Mr. Baldwin in another town. Therein it was said that that entertainment by Mr. Baldwin was an illusion, and thereupon the editor of Truth said he should not enquire further into the matter. If Dr. Ormonde would have said that his entertainment was an illusion he (Mr. Jarrott) would not have taken action in the matter, but he would not do so.

The Reverend Jarrott took along a list of questions to the performance which were answered but he concluded that the whole thing was just a trick and that Dr Ormonde wasn't in league with the devil. Remarkably, the Reverend Jarrott's speech on the matter attracted as many people as Dr Ormonde's show had.

The *Hamilton Advertiser* mentioned the Ormonde family in September, 1897:

This celebrated American company paid Stonehouse a visit this week, and occupied the Public Hall on Wednesday and Thursday. The entertainment was of a very high order, the marvellous skill of Miss Lottie Ormonde on the violin perfectly delighting the people, but the most interesting part of the programme was the clairvoyant revelations of Miss Stella Ormonde, the precision and accuracy of which were truly astonishing. Numerous tests were made, all of which she came out of successfully. Another feature of the entertainment was Dr. Ormonde's trick, 'The Escaped Convict'.

Interestingly, the article refers to the family as being American.

In 1898, Dr Ormonde wrote a book entitled *Mystery Unveiled* which was published in Edinburgh.

By 1900, the Ormondes were touring Ireland and in October of that year appeared in the Town Hall, Sligo, for one night only. They were billed as coming 'direct from the front'. Lottie was described as a 'lightning calculator' and Stella as a 'Modern Witch of Endor'. The act now included Miss Minnie Baldwin (the 'American Minerva') and the Flying Mahatmas.

The *Dundee Evening Post* of Thursday, 24 October 1901 noted:

Last night, Perth received a visit from the famous Dr Ormonde and his company, the entertainment taking place in the City Hall. What was perhaps the outstanding feature of the programme was the marvellous performance given by the hypnotised Mdlle. Stella Ormonde, who divulged the secrets of the whereabouts of missing friends and past and future events with remarkable skill. Mdlle. Ormonde earned for herself the plaudits of a large audience. Miss Lottie Ormonde, with the violin, captivated the audience, playing with fine purity of tone. She had to respond to several encores. Mr Fred Ormonde gave an exhibition of cartoon sketching, and although his drawings of the South African Generals were not of the highest order, they were performed with remarkable rapidity and reflected credit for his talents as a rapid sketcher. Besides several other interesting items, a cinematograph exhibition was also given, which proved a huge success. The entertainment was an excellent one all through.

When the Ormonde family appeared at Dungannon, it appeared that the 'Vivo-Tableaux' was more of a draw than they were. Audiences were now fascinated by any kind of moving pictures.

The *Tyrone Courier* of Thursday, 23 January 1902 noted:

Dr. and Mdlle. S. Ormonde, the 'Mahatmas of the West,' and their 'Sunflower Coterie,' with the Vivo-Tableaux, which has lately been creating a furore of excitement in London and Paris, are announced to appear in the Foresters Hall, on Monday, 27th January. In speaking of the entertainment, a contemporary says:

'The chief attraction of the evening is the Vivo-Tableaux which has justly won a reputation for the excellence and remarkable vividness of the animated pictures of the latest scenes of the Boer and China wars, depicting guns and troops in actual action. A stirring spectacle of a complete Spanish bull-fight, full of exciting action, is then produced as performed in the Grand Plaza de Torres de Madrid, the daring and exciting performances completely amazing and thrilling the audience. Following this in rapid succession are the wrestlers, the wonderful Brahmia and the fairy princess, the great prize-fight between John Bull and Kruger, and innumerable sensational and amusing animated pictures.

Dr. Ormonde showed himself a complete master of hypnotism. The entertainments are of a high-class variety nature, and include brilliant violin selections by Miss Lottie Ormonde, which are vociferously encored. Miss Lottie plays upon a rare and valuable old Russian violin, made by the famous S. Kiaposse, St Petersburg, and valued at £650. Its characteristics are great power and wonderful sweetness of tone, and it is stated to be equal in some respects to the historic fiddle said to have been gambled away by Paganini. Dr. Ormonde proves himself a Heller, Houdin and Anderson rolled into one, and amazes and delights while he mystifies his audience like a Mahatmas. Mr Fred Ormonde gives an admirable exposition of ventriloquism and sketches with amazing rapidity portraits of leading social and political celebrities, landscapes and sea pieces, while Mr Percy Ormonde is an adept on the Hungarian cimbalon. But excellent as all the parts of the entertainment are, the real interest is centred on the Doctor and Mdlle. Stella Ormonde in their marvellous clairvoyancy. Mdlle Stella enters into a mesmeric or clairvoyant condition, and then

A portrait of Dr Ormonde featured in the *Edinburgh Evening News* of Wednesday, 29 January 1902 on the announcement of his death.

begins the marvellous revelations. The Ormondes undoubtedly present a great entertainment, and we feel sure they will be welcomed with a crowded house in Dungannon.

The death of Dr Ormonde was reported in the *Motherwell Times* of Friday, 31 January 1902:

Dr Ormonde, the hypnotist and entertainer, and the father of the talented Ormonde family, died at his residence, 3 Antigua Street, Edinburgh, on Tuesday, after a long illness. Deceased was an Orcadian, born at Kirkwall, and travelled considerably abroad, throughout America, Australia and India giving entertainments, and meeting with much success wherever he appeared. He was the author of *Mystery Unveiled, Leaves from a Showman's Diary, How to become a Hypnotist*, and several other works. Dr Ormonde regularly visited Motherwell, and his entertainments in the Town Hall were very popular.

Confusion arises from this newspaper cutting as, in the *Ballymena Observer* of Friday, 18 August 1905, over three years later, Dr Ormonde and his troupe are playing at Ballymena with Houdini on the bill. Dr Ormonde continued to tour until October 1914 and then disappeared. It would appear that his son, Percy, took on the role and name of 'Dr Ormonde' and carried on the show.

According to an advert in the *Ballymena Observer* of Friday, 18 August 1905, Houdini appeared at the Protestant Hall, Ballymena for one night only on Friday 25 August, 1905. He was second on the bill after Dr Ormonde who was described as 'King Hypnotist and Monarch of the Marvellous'. The show promised that Houdini would escape from a large iron cage after being securely bound with handcuffs and leg-irons. His show featured an act called the 'Tiger's Den'.

Houdini and the Ormonde's were still in Northern Ireland in September and the *Era* of Saturday, 16 September 1905, reported:

The new town hall in Newry was packed on Monday to see Dr and Mdlle Ormonde. The Doctor entirely baffled his audience with his numerous tricks and illusions and in his hypnotic exhibition amazed all and proved himself a veritable healer. Mr Fred Ormonde, the lightning cartoonist, did some excellent sketches, that of 'Tim' Healy KC MP, being very well received. Houdini, the marvellous handcuff king, went through his remarkable performance with chains, irons and padlocks. Mdlle Ormonde, the 'World's Wonder', entered into a trance and astonishing her hearers by her remarkable and correct revelations. Miss Ormonde gave a violin solo, for which she received an ovation, and the entertainment concluded with some excellent animated pictures which were up to date and well received.

Oddly, it seems, Dr Ormonde and his family were more of a draw in Northern Ireland than Houdini himself.

By 1909, Fred Ormonde was offering his services as a conjurer and clairvoyant for evening parties in the small ads of *The Scotsman* although Dr Ormonde and his family continued to perform until the outbreak of the First World War.

An advert announcing the appearance of Dr Ormonde at the Protestant Hall, Ballymena in August 1905.

Chapter Sixteen

Dr Walford Bodie

Walford Bodie was born Samuel Murphy Bodie in Aberdeen on 11 June 1869. He toured as a hypnotist, magician, ventriloquist and 'electrician'. Like many of the performers of the day, he assumed the title 'Dr' although he had no medical training. At the age of 14, he became an apprentice at the National Telephone Company.

His first public performance was at Stonehaven Town Hall in 1884 when he was 15 years old. In 1903, he appeared at the Britannia Theatre, London, his first appearance in the city. He quickly built up a reputation for using electricity in his act and was labelled the 'British Edison'.

Charlie Chaplin impersonating Dr Walford Bodie.

Dr Walford Bodie's show at the Palace Theatre, Glasgow in November 1905.

I LEAD. FOLLOW WHO CAN.
THE MONEY MAGNET. THE RECORD BREAKER. THE MAN WITH THE MAGIC TOUCH.

DR. WALFORD BODIE,
M.D.,

THE MIRACLE WORKER OF THE NORTH, THE GREAT HEALER,
the World's Greatest Exponent of

BLOODLESS SURGERY,

Hypnotist, Electrician, and Scientist, introducing his Gorgeous Fit-up of Electrical Apparatus, purchased at a Cost of over £2,000.

Now playing to Record Business in BONNIE SCOTLAND, turning Hundreds away Nightly. Took £415 at GAIETY THEATRE, LEITH, and this my Seventh Visit. Finished on the Saturday night, at the CENTURY THEATRE, MOTHERWELL, to £100 1-., and I still hold the Record, playing this week to overflowing houses at THEATRE ROYAL, COATBRIDGE, beating all my previous Records, and this my Eighth Visit.

Owing to the New Theatre, Kirkcaldy, not being ready, I will take a week's rest at my Beautiful Highland Home, Macduff, N.B., the only Week I have Vacant for Two Years. Thanks to R. C. Buchanan, Esq., for offer of a Date at any of his Theatres for next week. Also Thanks to George Adney Payne, Esq., for offer of £220 Salary for my own Act alone for next week in London, but have made up my mind to take One Week at Home with my kiddies, inhaling the ozone, and having a quiet dram on my own, and I deserve it. How many of my friends would throw away £220 !

OPEN AT

PALACE THEATRE, GLASGOW,
NOV. 7.

BODIE OF MACDUFF.

All letters address next week to Bohemia House, Macduff, N.B.

An advert for Dr Walford Bodie's show at the Palace Theatre, Glasgow in November 1904.

His act was billed as 'Electric Wizardry' and included a section called 'bloodless surgery', which claimed to cure many ailments using hypnotism and electricity. This upset the medical profession and led to many complaints from them over the years. His show also included mock executions which involved a replica of the electric chair.

At the end of each show, his assistant, 'La Belle Electra' would strap him into the chair where he would, apparently, have 30,000 volts passed through him, lighting up sixteen lamps and two light bulbs in his hands. It was all an illusion but greatly delighted the audience. He was immensely popular in the early 1900s and his act inspired both Charlie Chaplin and Harry Houdini.

Bodie described himself as the 'Most Remarkable Man on Earth'. At one point, he was the highest paid entertainer of his day. He offered a 'cure-all' service and his poster carried the phrase 'bring your cripples'.

In 1886, he met his future wife, Jeannie Henry, at a show in Banff.

A caricature of Dr Walford Bodie from 1905.

A poster advertising the coming of Dr Walford Bodie to Glasgow in September 1905.

After they married, he had a home built for them in Skene Street, MacDuff which he called 'The Manor House'. Jeannie assisted him on stage under the name, Princess Rubie. Her older sisters also appeared on stage, most notably Isabella, who appeared as 'La Belle Electra'. Her other sister, Mary, appeared as Mystic Marie.

Walford Bodie and his wife had three children, a daughter named Jeannie and a son Albert who later also became an illusionist, as well as a son, Samuel, who became a real doctor and worked as a medical practitioner at Edinburgh Hospital.

In 1905, his stage 'cures' were so well-known that he was made a Freeman of the City of London. From this, he set up the 'Bodie Electric Drug Company' and published a book on the subject much to the dismay of the medical profession who labelled him a 'quack'. Bodie was taken to court several times. In 1905, the medical profession objected to him using the initials MD at the end of his name. He claimed that this carried no medical significance and actually stood for 'Merry Devil'.

The *Motherwell Times* of Friday, 14 July 1905 reported on his court appearance:

Mr Walford Bodie, who is pretty well known in Scotland for his hypnotic entertainments, was fined £5 and five guineas costs on Monday at Lambeth Police Court, at the instance of the Medical Defence Union, for illegal use of the title and description of 'Doctor', 'M.D.' and 'Surgeon' while performing at the Camberwell Palace Theatre of Varieties. The prosecution urged that Mr Bodie was treating people on the stage and proclaiming himself a qualified doctor, adopting a course degrading the medical profession. The defence was that, though Mr Bodie was not qualified in this country and treated persons by hypnotism and surgery, he held medical degrees which in America would entitle him to describe himself as he had done. In the bills issued for the Camberwell Palace

An advert for Dr Walford Bodie's show at the Tivoli, Leeds in March 1905.

A serious portrait of Dr Walford Bodie, complete with upturned moustache.

A theatre poster promoting Dr Walford Bodie MD, 'The Modern Miracle Worker.'

performance, however, the letters 'U.S.A.' had been omitted. The case, in the magistrate's opinion, was one for the mitigated penalty, and he adjudged accordingly.

In 1906, Chaplin imitated Bodie on stage and continued to do so in Hollywood. Bodie and Houdini became great friends.

In 1909, Bodie was sued by his former pupil, Charles Irving, for alleged misrepresentation. He was ordered by the courts to pay him £1,000. Bodie had taken money from Irving and had promised to show him the ways of 'electric surgery' which Irving had thought was real but later discovered otherwise. Also in 1909, Bodie's daughter, Jeannie, died at just 18 years old. He later paid for a fountain to be erected in Macduff as a memorial.

A photo of a dapper Dr Walford Bodie, complete with trademark moustache.

As noted, Bodie greatly upset members of the medical profession and the *Sheffield Evening Telegraph* of Friday, 12 November 1909 carried the story of a riot at the Glasgow Coliseum:

The resentment manifested against 'Dr.' Walford Bodie at the Glasgow Coliseum music-hall this week culminated last night in an attack upon the stage of the theatre by a band of students, with the result that the performer was compelled to retreat and the second house had to be abandoned. The disturbance was of so serious character that several of the students who engineered it were taken into custody.

The attack (says the Glasgow correspondent of the *Manchester Guardian*) was professedly organised for the purpose of avenging the insult which had been levelled at the students in describing them as 'Gilmore Hill Carnegieites'. Notices were posted at the University calling upon the students to attend this evening's performance at the Coliseum in a body. They marched to the hall 500 strong, having booked a sufficient number of seats in the afternoon. The early part of the entertainment was gone through with ample indication that a storm was brewing. The students, seated mostly in the stalls, were in a hilarious mood, and when Bodie's turn was announced they broke into a chorus, 'For he's a merry devil,' to the tune of 'For he's a jolly good fellow.' The orchestra had now retreated from their places.

When the curtain was raised, eggs, peasemeal and other missiles were showered upon the stage, and before the performer appeared, the scenery presented a woebegone appearance. The bags of peasemeal and flour burst upon the effects which Bodie employs in his performance and sent up clouds of white and bluish mixture into the air, which was polluted with the odour of bad eggs. Bodie was seen standing in the wings. The undergraduates shouted to him to

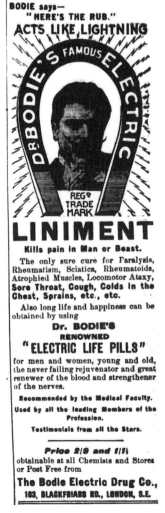

An advert from 1907 promoting 'Dr Bodie's Famous Electric Liniment'. It claimed to kill pain in man or beast and cured a whole range of illnesses from paralysis to coughs. Also available were 'Dr Bodie's Electric Life Pills'.

show himself, and at last he appeared, accompanied by 'La Belle Electra'. They were greeted by a shower of missiles, but Bodie smiled and tried to begin his performance. He, however, persuaded the lady to retire.

The greatest excitement prevailed in the theatre. Several students climbed over the orchestra with the object of reaching the stage, but before they gained it, the fireproof curtain was promptly lowered. This now became the target for peasemeal, eggs, and other things. The students were determined, however, to get beyond the footlights. They produced knives and saws, and soon rent huge gashes in the curtain. The stage staff tried to resist the attack pushing broomsticks and other weapons through the holes, and they succeeded in bowling over several students in the orchestra.

Matters were assuming a very alarming aspect when the heads of several policemen peered through the holes in the curtain, and before the attacking party realised what had occurred they found themselves surrounded by a large body of police, who had come from the back of the stage as well as from the auditorium. Four of the ringleaders of the disturbance were arrested and taken to the Police Station. In consequence of the disorderly proceedings the management deemed it advisable to cancel the usual second performance. When the police made their appearance in the Coliseum a struggle ensued, students being hurled over into the orchestra. Fighting took place for some time in all parts of the house. The students afterwards proceeded to the Police Office to protest against the arrest of their comrades. Disturbances also took place in another part of the city, and the police had to draw their truncheons, some students being injured.

The students had chanted at the magician 'Bodie, Bodie, Quack, Quack, Quack.' Three days later, his London home was attacked by further students and an effigy of Bodie was burned in the street. The protests were described as the worst student riots in Scottish history. Bodie was greatly affected by the riots and was almost destroyed by them. He took a year off to recover while he wrote books and made plans to reinvent his act.

In 1912, Bodie drew larger audiences than Harry Lauder when he appeared in Aberdeen.

The *Aberdeen Press and Journal* of Monday, 3 March 1913 carried a report of a later student disruption:

One of the principal performers at the Lyceum Theatre, Goran, last week, was Dr Walford Bodie. On Friday night, a considerable body of students succeeded in getting into the theatre and occupying the stalls, from which they kept up a lively commentary upon the proceedings.

When Dr Bodie appeared in highland costume to proceed with his entertainment, the students frequently interrupted and on his attempting to address the audience, he was greeted with ironical cries of 'Hear, hear'.

At the close of his performance, he addressed the students and invited them to send a deputation of six to examine the diplomas which entitled him to use the honorary title of doctor. A deputation of the students was formed and thereafter the proceedings were comparatively quiet. Superintendent Mennie, of the Goran Police Division, had received word of the projected demonstration of the students and he had a large staff of constables inside and outside the theatre. No action was called for, however, by the police, as the students dispersed quietly at the close.

In 1913, Bodie was back in court over action again brought by former pupil, Charles Irving. The *Leeds Mercury* of Thursday, 27 November 1913 reported:

Mr. Walford Bodie, 'the bloodless surgeon', of music-hall fame, was one of the defendants in an action brought before Mr. Justice Scrutton at the West Riding Assizes at Leeds, yesterday.

The plaintiffs were Charles Henry Irving, motor engineer, of Leeds, and Theo. Jones Matthias, another Leeds motor engineer, and the defendants were Samuel Murphy Bodie and Wm. Lovell Collins, from whom were claimed damages for libel.

Mr. Frank Mellor, who appeared for the plaintiffs, said the only question for the jury to decide was the amount of the damages.

In 1906, said counsel, the plaintiff Irving, who was then under twenty-one years of age, went to one of Bodie's performances, and was so impressed with it that he desired to associate himself with the show. An agreement was entered into, under which Bodie, in consideration of the payment of a thousand pounds, undertook to teach the plaintiff the business of a 'hypnotist, bloodless surgeon and medical electrical specialist'. The plaintiff was to receive a salary of two pounds a week.

At the same time, the other plaintiff, who was Mr. Irving's brother-in-law, was persuaded to enter into partnership with Bodie who was carrying on the business of manufacturing drugs and patent medicines, and in this case another thousand pounds was handed over to Bodie.

It was not long, said counsel, before Mr. Irving regretted his arrangement with Bodie, and in November, 1909, he brought an action to recover damages for fraudulent misrepresentation, the result being a verdict for the plaintiff for a thousand pounds. One of the witnesses in that action was the other defendant, Collins, the substance of whose evidence was that he had been

Bodie's assistant for fifteen years, and he was one of a number of paid men who sat among the audience and pretended to be independent people who were hypnotised and cured of various diseases.

At the commencement of 1912, it came to the knowledge of the two plaintiffs that the defendants were publishing a poster headed 'Startling Confession'. Justice at last for Dr. Walford Bodie. His good name now vindicated', and there followed a declaration, signed by Collins, in which he retracted everything said in the witness box, and asserted that the 'cruel and unwarrantable' case brought against Bodie was indirectly an attempt at blackmail. This placard was posted up on numerous theatres in South Wales, and was read to audiences.

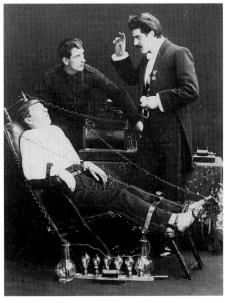

Dr Walford Bodie shown with his electric chair apparatus.

As soon as it came to the notice of the plaintiffs, they instituted proceedings for an interlocutory injunction restraining the defendants from issuing these statements, and Collins had since signed a statement that he signed the alleged confession at the request of the defendant Bodie, and when in a state of semi-drunkenness, and that he knew nothing of the alleged attempt at blackmail. No evidence was called for the defence, and Mr. Mortimer, who appeared for the defendants, confined his arguments to the question of damages.

The jury found for £100 damages for each of the plaintiffs, and his Lordship entered judgment accordingly. His Lordship also granted that the interlocutory injunction be made perpetual.

The court case not only showed Bodie in a bad light, for the way that he treated Charles Irving, but also revealed that all of the people who he had 'hypnotised', were paid to play along. One man testified that Bodie had paid him to come on stage struggling on crutches which were miraculously thrown away when Bodie 'cured' him.

Tragedy struck again in 1915 when Bodie's son, Albert, died aged 25. He had been a member of the Royal Society of Illusionists.

In 1916, during the First World War, the ship on which Bodie was travelling back from the Middle East, was torpedoed and sunk. Luckily, both himself and his touring company were safely rescued.

The *Aberdeen Weekly Journal* of Friday, 18 February 1916 reported:

Walford Bodie, the well-known 'electric wizard', who for the past three months has been touring South Africa along with his company of Scottish artistes, has been committed for trial at East London, South Africa, on a charge of pretending to be a physician.

Dr Walford Bodie's name is a household word in this country, which he has toured for the past twenty years both with his own company and as music-hall performer. His entertainment consists of hypnotism and electrical experiment which includes 'miraculous' cures on the stage.

As is well-known, this noted showman is a native of Aberdeen. His family residence is the Manor House, Macduff.

In 1920, Houdini gave Bodie a real electric chair which was used at Sing Sing prison.

Bodie continued to tour until the 1920s with the 'Bodie Show' which was very much variety based. By the 1930s, he owned a nightclub in London as well as a houseboat which he named after his former assistant, 'La Belle Electra'. He lived there with his second wife and had lavish parties whose guests included the future king, Edward VIII and his fiancée, Wallis Simpson. After the death of his first wife, Jeannie Henry, in 1931, Bodie, a well-known womaniser, married a 22-year-old showgirl called Florrie Robertshaw.

When depression hit in the mid-1930s, Bodie found himself performing at smaller venues. In 1939, while performing at Blackpool Pleasure Beach, he collapsed on stage and died several days after, aged 70.

News of his death was carried in the *Birmingham Mail* of Saturday, 21 October 1939 although he was mistakenly reported as being 68 years old:

'Dr.' Walford Bodie, for many years one of the most spectacular figures of the music hall stage, where he was known as the 'electrical wizard', has died at Blackpool, following an operation, at the age of 68. His appearances on the stage were almost invariably accompanied by a long line of cripples and persons suffering from paralysis, whom he treated in the presence of the audience.

In 1931, he retired to live in Macduff, in the north of Scotland, but the following year, in answer, he said, to the appeal of hundreds of former 'patients' he returned to the West End stage.

Dr. Bodie used to say that he did not charge his patients anything but that he had received from many of them tokens to the value of well over £5,000. At one time he worked with Sir Harry Lauder.

In one of the numerous law cases in which he was involved, a witness said he had been working with Dr. Bodie as a hypnotic subject. 'But 1 was never hypnotised', he added.

Dr. Bodie, who was a Scotsman, wrote a book, *How to Become a Mesmerist*, in which he said: 'I was originally intended for the Church, but theology had no charm for me. Then I started medicine, and graduated in that subject, and took my degree in dental surgery in the United States.'

These claims, he later admitted, were 'showman's lies'. So were statements that he had studied the occult in Paris, Vienna, China and Japan. 'I am very imaginative,' he said, 'I went there in my dreams.'

The 'M.D.' after his name, he said, meant 'Merry Devil'.

A portrait of an older Walford Bodie featured in the *Birmingham Mail* of Saturday, 21 October 1939.

Walford Bodie had many associations with the Midlands. His general manager for a period of 16 years was Mr. Lawson Trout, the Birmingham publicity agent, in whose possession is a cheque bearing Mr. Bodie's photograph issued by one of the Big Five and believed to be the first of its kind in the world. He paid many visits to Birmingham, and in the days before the last war he held the record for attendance at the Tivoli (now the Hippodrome), where he played for two consecutive weeks. During the last war, he played at the Hippodrome when it was under the control of the Draysey family, and held the record for the building with an attendance of 4,004 at the matinee. He came to a trades exhibition at Bingley Hall three years ago, and had also brought his sideshow to the Onion Fair, Aston. The funeral will take place on Tuesday at Macduff.

The *Aberdeen Press and Journal* of Saturday, 21 October 1939 paid its own tribute:

Dr Walford Bodie, who has died in hospital in Blackpool at the age of seventy following an operation, was one of the best known music hall entertainers who came to Aberdeen, his native city. He was one of the pioneers of showmanship, at least where the music halls were concerned, and his showmanship existed not only in his act but off stage as well. When he was visiting the town everyone knew about it. His posters were bigger and more animated than any others, and he was to be seen driving through the streets in a landau dressed in the 'dandiest' clothes of the day, gold monocle in eye, and groomed from top hat to buttoned boots. He advertised himself wherever he went.

His act, consisting of hypnotism, voltage and illusion, belonged to another day, and in latter years it probably did not produce the amazement of thirty to forty years ago. Then, there were noisy arguments as to what was real and what was trick, but in recent years the chief wonder of his act was himself. His entrance on the stage was the signal for the brass to blare, the drums to crash and the sparks to fly. His method was not to win his audiences, but to lord it over them – to make them feel honoured to be in such a great man's presence. His apparatus was the most elaborate and his manipulation of it was more so. If twenty flourishes of a wrist could be worked into the simple action of turning a handle they were there. The diamond on his ring was a dazzler and his astrakhan collar was a cape. All this no doubt belonged to another and more gullible age, but how it satisfied that age. Dr Bodie must have got immense inward pleasure from the gasps of astonishment that came from these audiences of thirty years ago, and when cinema and sophistication drove them to remoter districts, he followed them to smaller halls, making one-night 'stands' in the country districts.

He might have changed with the times for he was, we were told, outstanding at sleight of hand, but that was too quiet and too small for him.

When he was in Aberdeen early this year, the grand manner was still there. He carried a stick with an enormous gold top to it, his monocle shone as fiercely as ever, and the upturned moustache still bespoke the dandy.

Dr Bodie was educated at Robert Gordon's College and was intended for the ministry but preferred the stage. He took his degree as a doctor of dental surgery in America, and also studied in Paris and Vienna. An outstanding experience during his numerous tours was when, with his company, he was in the steamer *Arabia* which was torpedoed during the last war. He was one of the last to leave the vessel, and for three nights and three days he and his company were in a trawler in a terrible storm before they reached safety. For long he practised bloodless surgery and was said to get a salary of over £250 a week from it. Remarkable cures were credited to him. He had close links with Macduff. His first wife was a Macduff woman, and at one time he owned a number of properties there. For many years his home was in Macduff. He is survived by his second wife, who belongs to Leeds, and one son.

Walford Bodie was later buried in his hometown of Macduff. For many years afterwards, naughty children living in the town would be told by their parents that if they didn't behave, they would be 'visited by the ghost of Walford Bodie!'

Chapter Seventeen

John Henry Anderson

John Henry Anderson was born in 1814 and toured professionally as 'The Great Wizard of the North.' He was responsible for bringing street magic into theatres.

By the age of ten, Anderson was an orphan and first appeared on stage as part of a travelling dramatic company in 1830. At the age of 17, he started to perform magic and by the age of 23 was performing at the castle of Lord Panmure. His endorsement of Anderson encouraged him to go on tour, which he did for three years.

Anderson moved to London in 1840 and opened the New Strand Theatre. Sir Walter Scott was credited with giving him the name, 'The Great Wizard of the North'. Anderson proved very popular

An early sketch of John Anderson.

with audiences and was famous for his numerous successful performances of the Bullet Catch illusion, which later led to the death of Chung Ling Soo.

In 1842, Anderson married Hannah Longherst from Aberdeen, who assisted him on stage. In the following year, they had a son, John Henry Jr. Anderson also had a mistress, a Miss Prentice, who died in 1845 while giving birth to their son, Philip Prentice Anderson. He also later had two daughters who assisted in his shows, as well as a second illegitimate son with a member of his touring troupe.

Also in 1845, Anderson's second theatre, the City Theatre in Glasgow, was completed. However, by November, the theatre had burnt to the ground leaving Anderson with great financial losses. With the help of show-business friends, he launched a new show at London's Covent Garden in the following year.

In 1847, he toured Europe and met Tsar Nicholas at his last venue in St Petersburg. This led to him giving a command performance.

By 1849, Anderson had returned to London and performed in front of Queen Victoria and Prince Albert. In 1850, Anderson toured America, Canada, Australia, and Hawaii.

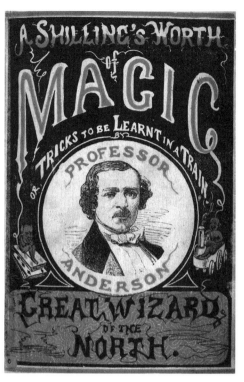

When he finally returned to Britain, he found that fellow magician Robert-Houdin had taken his place. This led Anderson to return to America in 1853 where he performed in Boston. He upset the temperance society there by performing an illusion that dispensed various alcoholic beverages.

In 1854, he performed a farewell performance in Aberdeen. However, due to the success of his show, he decided not to retire but to spend his time exposing spiritualism fraud. Together with his daughters, he performed shows showing the audience how fake spiritualists performed their act. He was one of the magicians who successfully exposed the Davenport Brothers.

A book cover of one of Professor Anderson's publications on magic.

The *Western Times* of Saturday, 4 February 1854 carried a story about Professor Anderson and table-rapping:

Recently, at Edinburgh, Professor Anderson gave his audience a specimen of table-rapping, which he showed to be a juggle, though in America thousands have been driven by it into a religious frenzy. After making the spirit, enclosed within a hollow table, obedient to his behests, to the satisfaction of his audience, he then removed the top of the table, and exhibited the said mysterious agent, which consisted of a small hammer similar to those which beat the hours of our clocks, and which was under the influence of a galvanic battery, connected to it by a wire conducted along the floor from beneath the stage.

His popular show appeared at the Lyceum in London before moving to Covent Garden in 1855. In 1856, after a gala performance, the theatre caught fire destroying all of Anderson's properties, bankrupting him for the second time in his professional career. For a while he became an actor before, in 1859, he commenced another world tour. His second daughter, Alice Hannah, assisted him, appearing on stage as Flora Anderson. She helped him with the Magic Portfolio and Hindu Decapitation illusions and also sang.

John Henry Anderson Jr left the troupe in 1862 at the age of 18 to tour independently as a conjurer. This led to an argument between father and son and they never spoke to each other again. In 1864, Anderson returned to England by which time he was greatly in debt. He toured again in 1866.

An article entitled 'Who is Professor Anderson?' appeared in the *Preston Chronicle* of Saturday, 19 November 1870. It read:

Who is Professor Anderson? The Great Wizard of the North, to whom that John Anderson in his showman's getup.

distinctive title was ascribed by Scotland's greatest author. The only true and original Wizard of the British Isles, who for nearly forty years has sustained a reputation unparalleled in the annals of Natural and Scientific Magic, and of whom it has been written, 'No other star disputes his throne, He reigns unrivalled and alone.' The great instructor of the young, of whom (during his extended career), no less than one million and a half belonging to various public and charitable institutions have been gratuitously entertained by him. The professional man who has continually sought to combine amusement with instruction, and while producing an entertainment fraught with much delight and enjoyment, remembering that coupled with amusement there can always be judiciously and prominently presented experiments at once illustrative of science, instructive while pleasing, and calculated to stimulate thought. The great demolisher in this country of the debasing system of Spiritualism unhappily so prevalent in America where it was also exposed by him, and in his conflicts with the Davenport Brothers and other propagandists of this modern superstition, the means of preventing its spread. The Wizard whose magic wand has directed into the coffers of many of the charitable Institutions and hospitals at home and abroad, irrespective of party or religion, vast sums of money; his own published and acknowledged contributions exceeding six thousand pounds.

Who is Miss Anderson? The only living lady gifted with the power of 'Second Sight', and whose muemonical capacity illustrates in a remarkable manner to what excellence the faculty of the memory may be cultivated. Her 'Second Sight', 'Feats of Memory', and exemplifications of Retro-Reminiscent Orthography, have been declared by the highest literary and scientific authorities to be so totally inexplicable, so perfectly marvellous and incomprehensible, that no effort on the part of an audience to clear the matter up could be successful by any process of reasoning.

Who is Miss Lizzie Anderson? The only European lady who has absolutely eclipsed the Japanese in the perfect manipulation of the beautiful Butterfly Trick, which she performs nightly with grace and dexterity.

What is the World of Magic? An entertainment for many years identified with the name of the Great Wizard of the North, which has been witnessed almost in every part of the habitable globe by admiring audiences, amounting in the aggregate up to the present time to upwards of seven millions: an entertainment baffling to ordinary mortals, exciting the wonder and admiration of every spectator, unique and of a most enjoyable character. It has been declared by a leading paper of the present day, to be unexceptional in every respect, coming up to the poet's ideal of what 'leisure hours demand', and affording ease in an extraordinary degree, instruction and amusement hand in hand.

Why does Professor Anderson visit Preston? To bid adieu to those remaining friends who welcomed him there on the occasion of his first visit 35 years ago, and to those who again so warmly supported him on his last visit 20 years since, as well as to prove to the present generation not only that his miraculous powers are unchanged, but that during two tours round the world and preparatory to undertaking a third, he has been able to add new and startling illusions, the result of his many discoveries and inventions in the field of Natural Magic.

Professor Anderson continued to tour, mainly in England, until he died,

Houdini visiting the grave of John Anderson, the 'Wizard of the North.'

four years later. The *Western Times* of Friday, 6 February 1874 carried a report of Anderson's death:

> Professor Anderson, 'the Wizard of the North', died on Tuesday at Darlington. He was sixty years of age and was born at Kincardine, Aberdeenshire. Last week, he was announced to perform at the Central Hall, Darlington, but he could not carry out his engagement, and he gradually sank. He went round the world three times in the practice of his art as a prestidigitant.

While in Aberdeen, Houdini visited the grave of John Anderson which was located within St Nicholas's Churchyard. Houdini was born in the same year as Anderson's death and was said to have been inspired by him. When Anderson's grave fell into disrepair, Houdini promised to pay for its upkeep.

Will Goldston mentioned Houdini's need to find graves of deceased magicians in his book *Sensational Tales of Mystery Men*:

> I have already made some reference to Houdini's love of publicity. It was his very life blood. He invented so many schemes for bringing his name before the public that I could fill several volumes on those alone. Some of them failed, most of them succeeded. Had they not done so, he might easily have died a poor and unknown man. Harry was not blind to the value of sentimental publicity. One of his favourite schemes was to hunt out the graves of any magicians who had lived in the particular town or district in which he was appearing. Then, accompanied by an army of press photographers, he would take a huge wreath to the graveside, standing bareheaded whilst his photograph was taken. On the following day, his likeness would appear in the papers with such words as 'Great Magician pays homage to a departed conjurer.' This idea tickled Harry immensely, and incidentally had the desired effect of increasing his popularity.
>
> When he was performing in Paris before the war, he decided to carry out this same programme, and accordingly hunted up the grave and records of Robert-Houdin, the eminent French illusionist. He went even further, and inquired for the whereabouts of Houdin's surviving relatives. To his utter astonishment, these good people refused to meet him, and informed him in a manner which left no room for doubt, that they wished to have nothing to do with him.

Chapter Eighteen

Jean-Eugène Robert-Houdin

Robert-Houdin is considered to be the father of modern magic. His spectacular illusions paved the way for future magicians and illusionists such as Houdini, Chung Ling Soo and The Great Lafayette.

Jean-Eugène Robert-Houdin was born in Blois, France on 7 December 1805. His father, Prosper Robert, was renowned for his watch making skills in his hometown of Blois. His mother, Marie-Catherine Guillon, died when he was a child. At the age of 11, Robert-Houdin was sent to the University of Orléans, 35 miles away from his home. He graduated aged 18 and returned home to Blois. His father wanted him to be a lawyer but Robert-Houdin had decided to become a watchmaker.

During the mid-1920s, he bought a book about watch making but when he returned home, he discovered that he had a two-volume set about magic called *Scientific Amusements*. Rather than taking the books back, he studied them and became fascinated with magic and illusion. He soon took instruction from an amateur magician, paying a man called Maous from Blois ten francs for a series of lessons in the art of magic. He continued with watch making while performing magic in his spare time.

Later, he joined an amateur acting troupe and performed at parties as a professional magician. While at a party, he met the daughter of a Parisian watchmaker, Monsieur Jacques François Houdin, who also came from Blois. His daughter's name was Josèphe Cecile Houdin, and they wed on 8 July, 1830. Jean hyphenated his own name to hers and became Robert-Houdin.

Soon after, he moved to Paris where he worked for his father-in-law in his watch making shop. Nearby was a shop which sold magic tricks which Robert-Houdin visited often and there he met fellow magicians. The shop was owned by Papa Roujol and it was there that Robert-Houdin discovered the workings of many of the mechanical tricks of the day and learnt how to improve them. He built his own mechanical figures including a singing bird, a dancer on a tightrope and an automaton using cups and balls. His most famous automaton was of a writing and drawing figure which he displayed before King Louis Philippe and later sold to P.T. Barnum.

Tragedy struck on 19 October, 1843, when Robert-Houdin's wife died, at the age of 32. He was left with three children and in August of the following year he

A poster advertising Harmington at 'Du Théâtre Robert-Houdin.' Harmington was a professional French magician who appeared at Robert-Houdin's theatre in 1886. He was born Charles Rey in 1860 and died in 1947.

A theatre poster promoting Robert-Houdin and his decapitation illusion.

married François Marguerite Olympe Braconnier, who was ten years younger than himself.

He worked on constructing equipment for his own use rather than selling it to others and the income from the shop and his new inventions gave him enough money to experiment on new illusions. He was backed by Count de l'Escalopier, who advanced him 15,000 francs to work on his magic show. He rented a suite of rooms at the Palais Royal and employed men to redesign the old assembly room into a theatre. It was redecorated white with gold trim. Drapes and candelabras were added throughout, and included stage furniture in the style of Louis XV.

On 3 July, 1845, Robert-Houdin opened his new 200-seat theatre, which he called 'Soirées Fantastiques'. The show proved to be a disaster and Robert-Houdin suffered from stage fright. He thought of closing the theatre but in the end decided to continue. He gained confidence with every show and as he got better, he began to receive critical acclaim. However, with small attendance figures, he struggled to keep the theatre open and met expenses by selling three houses that his mother had left him.

By the following year, he had invented a new trick which he called 'Second Sight'. This proved immensely popular and drew large audiences to the theatre. The trick involved Robert-Houdin's son, Emile, being blindfolded and stepping out into the audience and successfully identifying objects which were held up. The act caused a sensation. People suspected that Robert-Houdin was passing a code to his son when he poked him so in future performances, he simply rang a bell before his son described the objects held up in great detail.

Another illusion was the 'Ethereal Suspension.' He convinced audience members that by breathing in ether they could become as light as a balloon. He placed three stools on the stage and his youngest son, Eugène, stood on the one in the middle. When his father instructed him, he stretched out his arms. Two canes were placed on top of the stools and under Eugène's arms. Robert-Houdin produced a vial of ether and waved it under his son's nose. When the stool was taken away from his son's feet, he hung there limp as one of the canes was removed leaving him dangling by one arm. Robert-Houdin then lifted his son using his little finger, into a horizontal position. When he let go, the boy was left suspended in mid-air.

Other illusions included 'The Marvellous Orange Tree,' 'Robert-Houdin's Portfolio' and 'The Light and Heavy Chest'. His theatre became the place for magic enthusiasts to visit. Herrmann, a well-known French magician, attended the Palais Royal often. Soon Robert-Houdin was performing to the Paris elite and King Louis Philippe rented out the place for a private performance. After the triumph of his performance at the Royal Palace, in 1847, the king decided that he must see Robert-Houdin perform at the Palais Royal. Louis-Philippe's reign ended in the following February following a revolution which terminated their association.

Robert-Houdin made his debut in England at the St James's Theatre in April 1848 and appeared there three times a week. An advert for the show read:

Robert-Houdin will have the honour to resume his seances at the St. James's Theatre during the ensuing week, and will continue to present his Soirees Fantastiques every Tuesday, Thursday, and Saturday, until the end of the Christmas vacations. The programme will include numerous experiments, entirely new, composed and invented by Robert-Houdin expressly for live performances. Boxes and Stalls may be secured at Mr. Mitchell's Royal Library, 33, Old Bond-street, and the Box Office of the Theatre, from eleven till five o'clock.

Unhappily, he found that Compars Herrmann was already performing in England and billing himself as 'The Premier Prestidigitateur of France'. He was also using pirate versions of Robert-Houdin's stock illusions.

The *Morning Chronicle* of Friday, 2 June 1848 reported:

Robert-Houdin performing on stage as featured in the *London Illustrated News* of Saturday, 23 December 1848.

We last evening paid a visit to Mr. Robert-Houdin, the new miracle-worker, at the St. James's Theatre. We have seen many conjurors in our time; but we certainly never saw one who came up to this one. His tricks with cards, boxes, rings, birds, fishes, orange-trees, clocks, etc were endless in variety, and accomplished with a precision and grace which defied all criticism. One of his most remarkable scenes was called 'Le Carton de Robert Houdin' – a plain, fat portfolio, out of which he brought four doves, a lady's bonnet, and several other things, ending with a good-sized bird cage, containing live canaries. Another, which afforded the most complete delight to the audience, particularly those in the pit, was the 'Bouteille Inepuisable,' a common green bottle, from which he poured out for the company endless glasses of any liquors they liked to call for. Cognac, Maraschino, Curacao, Kirschwasser, eau de Vanille, gin, and innumerable other liquors were called for by the audience, supplied as quick as thought, and evidently relished by the recipients. But the most surprising parts of the performance were the feats of second-sight by Mr. Houdin's son. With his eyes bandaged, seated on the stage, he described without an instant's hesitation any article which was put into his father's hand by anyone in the body of the house. However this may have been managed, the rapidity and neatness with which it was accomplished were such as deservedly to elicit the applause of the audience. The concluding effect was the suspension in the air, on the end of a stick, of the younger son of Mr. Houdin, under, it was said, the effect of the concentrated ether, but for this we have only 'the ghost's word'.

The house was fully attended, and the audience appeared delighted not less with the tricks themselves than the agreeable manner of Mr. Houdin during the performance.

Robert-Houdin proved a great success and completed a command performance for Queen Victoria in the same year. After touring England, he headed back to France and reopened his theatre. In 1850, he entrusted his brother-in law, Hamilton (Pierre Etienne Chocat), with the Palais Royal and toured France for the following two years before performing in Germany. He then returned to England where he performed more shows and appeared before Queen Victoria for a second time.

Robert-Houdin in thoughtful mood.

After a brief tour of France, he decided to retire from performing at the age of 48. The theatre was now handed back to Hamilton who continued to put on shows to an enthusiastic public. After he retired, Robert-Houdin devoted his time to his inventions using electricity. He also spent a great deal of time writing. His home, le Prieuré (the Priory), was far advanced for its time and ran entirely on electricity.

In 1856, Louis-Napoleon asked him if he could help to pacify the tribes in French Algeria. Napoleon III was concerned about a religious group called the Marabouts. The Marabouts controlled their tribe with their fake magical abilities, and advised their leaders to break bonds with the French. Oddly, Napoleon chose Robert-Houdin to show them that French magic was more powerful.

A promotional photo of an older Robert-Houdin.

The magical mission started with a performance at the Bab Azoun Theatre in Algeria, where Robert-Houdin gave performances twice a week. He also performed before the country's tribal chiefs. He used the 'Light and Heavy Chest' illusion during these performances, but instead of playing for comedy as he had done in Paris, he played it straight. Robert-Houdin invited the strongest tribesman on stage and asked the Arabian to pick up the wooden chest placed on stage which he did easily. Robert-Houdin next announced that he was going to take away his strength. He waved a wand and stated, 'Contemplez! Maintenant vous êtes plus faible qu'une femme; essayez de soulever la boîte.' This translated to,

'Behold! Now you are weaker than a woman; try to lift the box.' The Arabian grabbed the handle of the chest, but could not move it. He continued to try to shift it before proceeding to rip it apart. Robert-Houdin had rigged the box to give the man an electic shock and suddenly he shouted out in pain and ran off the stage and out of the theatre.

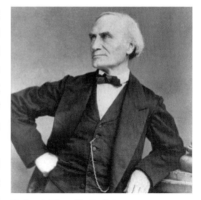

Robert-Houdin in later years.

After he had concluded his performances, he gave a special show for several of the chief men of the tribe. He was asked by Bou-Allem to the home of the head of the tribe where he was challenged to do a special trick. He agreed and invited one of the rebels to shoot at him with a marked bullet. He then caught this in his teeth. Bou-Allem presented him with a certificate while wearing a red robe symbolizing his loyalty to France. With the scroll praising his powers, Robert-Houdin returned to France and the mission was accomplished.

After his mission to Algeria, Robert-Houdin performed his last show at the Grand Théâtre in Marseille, before returning to his home in Saint-Gervais, near Blois, where he completed his memoirs, *Confidences d'un Prestidigitateur*. He also penned several books on the art of magic. For about fifteen years, he lived happily in retirement until the start of the Franco-Prussian War. His son Eugene was a captain in a Zouave regiment and on 6 August, 1870,

An older portrait of Robert-Houdin.

Robert-Houdin heard the news that he had been mortally wounded at the Battle of Worth. At the same time, Hessian soldiers captured Paris and Robert-Houdin was forced to hide his family in a cave close to his home.

Four days later, Robert-Houdin discovered that his son had died of his wounds. With the stress from that and the war, his health got worse and he developed pneumonia. He died as a result on 13 June, 1871, aged 65.

Bibliography

Books:

Beedham, Ann, *Randini, The Man Who Helped Houdini* (2009)

Cannell, J.C., *The Secrets of Houdini* (Dover Publications 1973)

Christopher, Milbourne, *Houdini: A Pictorial Biography* (1998)

Christopher, Milbourne, *Houdini: The Untold Story* (1969)

Christopher, Milbourne, *Magic: A Picture History* (1992)

Clempert, John, *Thrilling Episodes of John Clempert: The Shining Star of the Realms of Mystery* (1910)

Cox, Clinton, *Houdini* (Scholastic 2001)

Devant, David, *Our Magic* (1911)

Devant, David, *The Practice of Magic* (1911)

Devant, David, *The Theory in Magic* (1911)

Ernst, Bernard M.L., and Carrington, Hereward, *Houdini and Conan Doyle: The Story of a Strange Friendship* (1933)

Goldston, Will, *Exclusive Magical Secrets* (1912)

Goldston, Will, *The Magician's Annual* (1909)

Goldston, Will, *Sensational Tales of Mystery Men* (1928)

Hanzlik, Mick, *Houdini: A Biography* (2007)

Hanzlik, Mick, *Houdini's Mirror Handcuff Challenge 1904* (2007)

Hanzlik, Mick, *Looking Into The Mirror* (2007)

Hertz, Carl, *A Modern Mystery Merchant: The Trials, Tricks and Travels of Carl Hertz, the Famous American Illusionist* (1924)

Houdini, Harry, *A Magician among the Spirits* (1924)

Houdini, Harry, *The Adventurous Life of a Versatile Artist* (1922)

Kalush, William, and Sloman, Larry, *The Secret Life of Houdini* (Pocket Books 2007)

Tait, Derek, *The Great Houdini: His British Tours* (Pen and Sword 2017)

Woodward, Chris, *The London Palladium: The Story of the Theatre and Its Stars* (Jeremy Mills Publishing 2009)

Newspapers and Other Periodicals:

Aberdeen Press and Journal

Aberdeen Weekly Journal

Ballymena Observer
The *Bat*
Bell's Weekly Messenger
Birmingham Daily Gazette
Birmingham Mail
Brighton Gazette
Burnley Gazette
Burnley News
The *Conjurors' Magazine*
Cork Constitution
Coventry Evening Telegraph
Daily Express
Daily Illustrated Mirror
Daily Record
Derby Daily Telegraph
Derbyshire Times
Dundee Courier
Dundee Evening Post
Dundee Evening Telegraph
Edinburgh Evening News
Exeter and Plymouth Gazette
Fife Free Press and Kirkcaldy Guardian
Gloucester Citizen
Hamilton Advertiser
Hull Daily Mail
Ipswich Journal
Lancashire Evening Post
Leeds Mercury
Lincolnshire Chronicle
London and Provincial Entr'acte
London Daily News
London Evening Standard
Manchester Courier
Manchester Courier and Lancashire General Advertiser
Morning Chronicle
Motherwell Times
Nottingham Evening Post
Portsmouth Evening News
Preston Chronicle
The *Scotsman*

St James's Gazette
Sheffield Evening Telegraph
Sheffield Independent
Sporting Times
The *Stage*
Tyrone Courier
Weekly Dispatch
Western Daily Press
Western Morning News
Western Times
Yorkshire Evening Post

Recommended Websites:

John Cox's website at http://www.houdini-lives.com/Houdini_Lives/HOME.html
John Cox's 'Wild About Harry' blog at http://www.wildabouthoudini.com/
Marco Pusterla's blog at https://smallmagicollector.wordpress.com/
The Houdini Museum at https://houdinimuseum.wordpress.com/

Index